A NEW BLUEPRINT
FOR MANKIND

"In the Middle Ages it was the vision of the City of God that inspired us. Then, beginning in the 18th century, it was the vision of the City, of Earthly Progress, the sense that we must understand nature in order to dominate it. Now this has all ended in what looks like the Tower of Babel—that which was progressive in the Middle Ages and the 18th and 19th centuries has been lost. What we now desperately need is a synthesis between the faith of the late Middle Ages and the reason and science of the last two centuries. That's the only way I see that we can be saved from a sort of technocratic fascism."

—ERICH FROMM

BANTAM NEW AGE BOOKS

This important imprint includes books in a variety of fields and disciplines and deals with the search for meaning, growth and change. They are books that circumscribe our times and our future.

Ask your bookseller for the books you have missed.

ANIMAL DREAMING by Jim Nollman
THE ART OF BREATHING by Nancy Zi
BEYOND EINSTEIN: THE COSMIC QUEST FOR THE THEORY OF THE UNIVERSE by Dr. Michio Kaku and Jennifer Trainer
BEYOND THE QUANTUM by Michael Talbot
BEYOND SUPERNATURE by Lyall Watson
THE CASE FOR REINCARNATION by Joe Fisher
THE COMPLETE CRYSTAL GUIDEBOOK by Uma Silbey
THE COSMIC CODE by Heinz Pagels
CREATIVE VISUALIZATION by Shakti Gawain
THE DANCING WU LI MASTERS by Gary Zukav
DON'T SHOOT THE DOG: HOW TO IMPROVE YOURSELF AND OTHERS THROUGH BEHAVIORAL TRAINING by Karen Pryor
ECOTOPIA by Ernest Callenbach
EMMANUEL'S BOOK by Pat Rodegast and Judith Stanton
AN END TO INNOCENCE by Sheldon Kopp
ENTROPY by Jeremy Rifkin with Ted Howard
FOCUSING by Dr. Eugene T. Gendlin
THE HEART OF HEALING by Bruce Davis and Genny Wright Davis
I CHING: A NEW INTERPRETATION FOR MODERN TIMES by Sam Reifler
IF YOU MEET THE BUDDHA ON THE ROAD, KILL HIM! by Sheldon Kopp
IN SEARCH OF SCHRÖDINGER'S CAT by John Gribbin
IN SEARCH OF THE BIG BANG: QUANTUM PHYSICS AND COSMOLOGY by John Gribbin
IN SEARCH OF THE DOUBLE HELIX: QUANTUM PHYSICS AND LIFE by John Gribbin
INFINITY AND THE MIND by Rudy Rucker
KUNDALINI FOR THE NEW AGE/ Editor Gene Keiffer
THE LIVES OF A CELL by Lewis Thomas
MAGICAL CHILD by Joseph Chilton Pierce
MAGICAL CHILD MATURES by Joseph Chilton Pierce
THE MEDUSA AND THE SNAIL by Lewis Thomas
METAMAGICAL THEMAS: QUESTING FOR THE ESSENCE OF MIND AND PATTERN by Douglas R. Hofstadter
MIND AND NATURE by Gregory Bateson
THE MIND'S I by Douglas R. Hofstadter and Daniel C. Dennett
NATURAL ESP: THE ESP CORE AND ITS RAW CHARACTERISTICS by Ingo Swann
THE NEW STORY OF SCIENCE by Robert M. Augros and George N. Stanciu
THE OMEGA POINT: THE SEARCH FOR THE MISSING MASS AND THE ULTIMATE FATE OF THE UNIVERSE by John Gribbin
ORDER OUT OF CHAOS by Ilya Prigogine and Isabelle Stengers
ORIGINS: A SKEPTIC'S GUIDE TO THE CREATION OF LIFE ON EARTH by Robert Shapiro
PERFECT SYMMETRY by Heinz Pagels
PROSPERING WOMAN by Ruth Ross
THE REENCHANTMENT OF THE WORLD by Morris Berman
SCIENCE, ORDER AND CREATIVITY by David Bohm and F. David Peat
SHAMBHALA: THE SACRED PATH OF THE WARRIOR by Chogyam Trungpa
SPACE-TIME AND BEYOND (THE NEW EDITION) by Bob Toben and Fred Alan Wolf
STAYING SUPPLE by John Jerome
SUPERMIND by Barbara B. Brown
SYMPATHETIC VIBRATIONS: REFLECTIONS ON PHYSICS AS A WAY OF LIFE by K. C. Cole
SYNCHRONICITY: THE BRIDGE BETWEEN MATTER AND MIND by F. David Peat
THE TAO OF LEADERSHIP by John Heider
THE TAO OF PHYSICS (REVISED EDITION) by Fritjof Capra
TO HAVE OR TO BE? by Erich Fromm
THE TURNING POINT by Fritjof Capra
THE WAY OF THE SHAMAN: A GUIDE TO POWER AND HEALING by Michael Harner
ZEN AND THE ART OF MOTORCYCLE MAINTENANCE by Robert M. Pirsig

TO HAVE OR TO BE?
ERICH FROMM

A BANTAM NEW AGE BOOK

BANTAM BOOKS
NEW YORK · TORONTO · LONDON · SYDNEY · AUCKLAND

TO HAVE OR TO BE?
*A Bantam Book / published by arrangement with
Harper & Row, Publishers, Inc.*

PRINTING HISTORY
Harper & Row edition published October 1976
*A Selection of Psychotherapy & Social Science Book Center,
December 1976; Library of Human Behavior, January 1977 and
Psychology Today Book Club, February 1977.*
*Alternate Selections of Literary Guild of America and Mac-
millan Book Club, January 1977.*
Serialized in Journal of Vocational Behavior in 1977.
*Bantam edition / July 1981
5 printings through March 1988*

*New Age and the accompanying figure design as well as
the statement "a search for meaning, growth and change"
are trademarks of Bantam Books.*

*Bantam Books are published by Bantam Books, a division of
Bantam Doubleday Dell Publishing Group, Inc. Its trademark,
consisting of the words "Bantam Books" and the portrayal of
a rooster, is Registered in U.S. Patent and Trademark Office
and in other countries. Marca Registrada. Bantam Books,
666 Fifth Avenue, New York, New York 10103.*

Contents

World Perspectives
What This Series Means

It is the thesis of *World Perspectives* that man is in the process of developing a new consciousness which, in spite of his apparent spiritual and moral captivity, can eventually lift the human race above and beyond the fear, ignorance, and isolation which beset it today. It is to this nascent consciousness, to this concept of man born out of a universe perceived through a fresh vision of reality, that *World Perspectives* is dedicated.

My Introduction to this Series is not of course to be construed as a prefatory essay for each individual book. These few pages simply attempt to set forth the general aim and purpose of the Series as a whole. They try to point to the principle of permanence within change and to define the essential nature of man, as presented by those scholars who have been invited to participate in this intellectual and spiritual movement.

Man has entered a new era of evolutionary history, one in which rapid change is a dominant consequence. He is contending with a fundamental change, since he has intervened in the evolutionary process. He must now better appreciate this fact and then develop the wisdom to direct the process toward his fulfillment rather than toward his destruction. As he learns to apply his understanding of the physical world for practical purposes, he is, in reality, extending his innate capacity and augmenting his ability and his need to communicate as well as his ability to think and to create. And as a result, he is substituting a goal-directed evolutionary process in his struggle against environmental hardship for the slow, but effective, biological evolution which produced modern man through mutation and natural selection. By intelligent intervention in the evolutionary process man has greatly accelerated and greatly expanded the range of his possibilities. But he has not changed the basic fact that it remains a trial and error process, with the danger of taking paths that lead to sterility of mind and heart, moral apathy and intellectual inertia; and even producing social dinosaurs unfit to live in an evolving world.

Only those spiritual and intellectual leaders of our epoch who have a paternity in this extension of man's horizons are invited to participate in the Series: those who are aware of the truth that beyond the divisiveness among men there exists a primordial unitive power since we are all bound together by a common humanity more fundamental than any unity of dogma; those who recognize that the centrifugal force which has scattered and atomized mankind must be replaced by an integrating structure and process capable of bestowing meaning and purpose on existence; those who realize that science itself, when not inhibited by the limitations of its own methodology, when chastened and humbled, commits man to an indeterminate range of yet undreamed consequences that may flow from it.

Virtually all of our disciplines have relied on conceptions which are now incompatible with the Cartesian axiom, and with the static world view we once derived from it. For underlying the new ideas, including those of modern physics, is a unifying order, but it is not causality; it is purpose, and not the purpose of the universe and of man, but the purpose *in* the universe and *in* man. In other words, we seem to inhabit a world of dynamic process and structure. Therefore we need a calculus of potentiality rather than one of probability, a dialectic of polarity, one in which unity and diversity are redefined as simultaneous and necessary poles of the same essence.

Our situation is new. No civilization has previously had to face the challenge of scientific specialization, and our response must be new. Thus this Series is committed to ensure that the spiritual and moral needs of a man as a human being and the scientific and intellectual resources at his command for *life* may be brought into a productive, meaningful and creative harmony.

In a certain sense we may say that man now has regained his former geocentric position in the universe. For a picture of the Earth has been made available from distant space, from the lunar desert, and the sheer isolation of the Earth has become plain. This is as new and as powerful an idea in history as any that has ever been born in man's consciousness. We are all becoming seriously concerned with our natural environment. And this concern is not only the result of the warnings given by biologists, ecologists and conservationists. Rather it is the result of a deepening awareness that something new has happened, that the planet Earth is a unique and precious place. Indeed, it may not be a mere coincidence that this awareness should have been born at the exact moment when man took his first step into outer space.

This Series endeavors to point to a reality of which scientific theory has revealed only one aspect. It is the commitment to this reality that lends universal intent to a scientist's most original and solitary thought. By acknowledging this frankly we shall restore science to the great family of human aspirations by which men hope to fulfill themselves in the world community as thinking and sentient beings. For our problem is to discover a principle of differentiation and yet relationship lucid enough to justify and to purify scientific, philosophic and all other knowledge, both discursive and intuitive, by accepting their interdependence. This is the crisis in consciousness made articulate through the crisis in science. This is the new awakening.

Each volume presents the thought and belief of its author and points to the way in which religion, philosophy, art, science, economics, politics and history may constitute that form of human activity which takes the fullest and most precise account of variousness, possibility, complexity and difficulty. Thus *World Perspectives* endeavors to define that ecumenical power of the mind and heart which enables man through his mysterious greatness to re-create his life.

This Series is committed to a re-examination of all those sides of human endeavor which the specialist was taught to believe he could safely leave aside. It attempts to show the structural kinship between subject and object; the indwelling of the one in the other. It interprets present and past events impinging on human life in our growing World Age and world consciousness and envisages what man may yet attain when summoned by an unbending inner necessity to the quest of what is most exalted in him. Its purpose is to offer new vistas in terms of world and human development while refusing to betray the intimate correlation between universality and individuality, dynamics and form, freedom and destiny. Each author deals with the increasing realization that spirit and nature are not separate and apart; that intuition and reason must regain their convergence as the means of perceiving and fusing inner being with outer reality.

World Perspectives endeavors to show that the conception of wholeness, unity, organism is a higher and more concrete conception than that of matter and energy. Thus an enlarged meaning of life, of biology, not as it is revealed in the test tube of the laboratory but as it is experienced within the organism of life itself, is attempted in this Series. For the principle of life consists in the tension which connects spirit with the realm of matter, symbiotically joined. The element of life is dominant in the very texture of nature, thus rendering life, biology, a transempirical science. The laws of life have their origin beyond their mere physical manifestations and compel us to consider their spiritual source. In fact, the widening of the conceptual framework has not only served to restore order within the respective branches of knowledge, but has also disclosed analogies in man's position regarding the analysis and synthesis of experience in apparently separated domains of knowledge, suggesting the possibility of an ever more embracing objective description of the meaning of life.

Knowledge, it is shown in these books, no longer consists in a manipulation of man and nature as opposite forces, nor in the reduction of data to mere statistical order, but is a means of liberating mankind from the destructive power of fear, pointing the way toward the goal of the rehabilitation of the human will and the rebirth of faith and confidence in the human person. The works published also endeavor to reveal that the cry for patterns, systems and authorities is growing less insistent as the desire grows stronger in both East and West for the recovery of a dignity, integrity and self-realization which are the inalienable rights of man who may not guide change by means of conscious purpose in the light of rational experience.

The volumes in this Series endeavor to demonstrate that only in a society in which awareness of the problems of science exists, can its discoveries start great waves of change in human culture, and in such a manner that these discoveries may deepen and not erode the sense of universal human community. The differences in the disciplines, their epistemological exclusiveness, the variety of historical experiences, the difference of traditions, of cultures, of languages, of the arts, should be protected and preserved. But the interrelationship and unity of the whole should at the same time be accepted.

The authors of *World Perspectives* are of course aware that the ultimate answers to the hopes and fears which pervade modern society rest on the moral fibre of man, and on the wisdom and responsibility of those who promote the course of its development. But moral decisions cannot dispense with an insight into the interplay of the objective elements which offer and limit the choices made. Therefore an understanding of what the issues are, though not a sufficient condition, is a necessary prerequisite for directing action toward constructive solutions.

Other vital questions explored relate to problems of international understanding as well as to problems dealing with prejudice and the resultant tensions and antagonisms. The growing perception and responsibility of our World Age point to the new reality that the individual person and the collective person supplement and integrate each other; that the thrall of totalitarianism of both left and right has been shaken in the universal desire to recapture the authority of truth and human totality. Mankind can finally place its trust not in a proletarian authoritarianism, not in a secularized humanism, both of which have betrayed the spiritual property right of history, but in a sacramental brotherhood and in the unity of knowledge. This new consciousness has created a widening of human horizons beyond every parochialism, and a revolution in human thought comparable to the basic assumption, among the ancient Greeks, of the sovereignty of reason; corresponding to the great effulgence of the moral conscience articulated by the Hebrew prophets; analogous to the fundamental assertions of Christianity; or to the beginning of the new scientific era, the era of the science of dynamics, the experimental foundations of which were laid by Galileo in the Renaissance.

An important effort of this series is to re-examine the contradictory meanings and applications which are given today to such terms as democracy, freedom, justice, love, peace, brotherhood and God. The purpose of such inquiries is to clear the way for the foundation of a genuine *world* history not in terms of nation or race or culture but in terms of man in relation to God, to himself, his fellow man and the universe, that reach beyond immediate self-interest. For the meaning of the World Age consists in respecting man's hopes and dreams which lead to a deeper understanding of the basic values of all peoples.

World Perspectives is planned to gain insight into the meaning of man, who not only is determined by history but who also determines history. History is to be understood as concerned not only with the life of man on this planet but as including also such cosmic influences as interpenetrate our human world. This generation is discovering that history does not conform to the social optimism of modern civlization and that the organization of human communities and the establishment of freedom and peace are not only intellectual achievements but spiritual and moral achievements as well, demanding a cherishing of the wholeness of human personality, the "unmediated wholeness of feeling and thought," and constituting a never-ending challenge to man, emerging from the abyss of meaninglessness and suffering, to be renewed and re-plenished in the totality of his life.

Justice itself, which has been "in a state of pilgrimage and crucifixion" and now is being slowly liberated from the grip of social and political demonologies in the East as well as in the West, begins to question its own premises. The modern revolutionary movements which have challenged the sacred institutions of society by protecting injustice in the name of social justice are here examined and re-evaluated.

In the light of this, we have no choice but to admit that the *un*freedom against which freedom is measured must be retained with it, namely, that the aspect of truth out of which the night view appears to emerge, the darkness of our time, is as little abandonable as is man's subjective advance. Thus the two sources of man's consciousness are inseparable, not as dead but as living and complementary, an aspect of that "principle of complementarity" through which Niels Bohr has sought to unite the quantum and the wave, both of which constitute the very fabric of life's radiant energy.

There is in mankind today a counterforce to the sterility and danger of a quantitative, anonymous mass culture; a new, if sometimes imperceptible, spiritual sense of convergence toward human and world unity on the basis of the sacredness of each human person and respect for the plurality of cultures. There is a growing awareness that equality may not be evaluated in mere numerical terms but is proportionate and analogical in its reality. For when equality is equated with interchangeability, individuality is negated and the human person transmuted into a faceless mask.

We stand at the brink of an age of a world in which human life presses forward to actualize new forms. The false separation of man and nature, of time and space, of freedom and security, is acknowledged, and we are faced with a new vision of man in his organic unity and of history offering a richness and diversity of equality and majesty of scope hitherto unprecedented. In relating the accumulated wisdom of man's spirit to the new reality of the World Age, in articulating its thought and belief, *World Perspectives* seeks to encourage a renaissance of hope in society and of pride in man's decision as to what his destiny will be.

Man has certainly contrived to change the environment, but subject to the new processes involved in this change, the same process of selection continues to operate. The environment has changed partly in a physical and geographical sense, but more particularly from the knowledge we now possess. The Biblical story of Adam and Eve contains a deep lesson, which a casual reading hardly reveals. Once the "fruit of the Tree of Knowledge" has been eaten, the world is changed. The new world is dictated by the knowledge itself, not of course by an edict of God. The Biblical story has further interest in that the new world is said to be much worse than the former idyllic state of ignorance. Today we are beginning to wonder whether this might not also be true. Yet we are uneasy, apprehensive, and our fears lead to the collapse of civilizations. Thus we turn to the truth that knowledge and life are indivisible, even as life and death are inseparable. We *are* what we know and think and feel; we are linked with history, with the world, with the universe, and faith in *Life* creates its own verification.

World Perspectives is committed to the recognition that all great changes are preceded by a vigorous intellectual re-evaluation and reorganization. Our authors are aware that the sin of *hubris* may be avoided by showing that the creative process itself is not a free activity if by free we mean arbitrary, or unrelated to cosmic law. For the creative process in the human mind, the developmental process in organic nature and the basic laws of the inorganic realm may be but varied expressions of a universal formative process. Thus *World Perspectives* hopes to show that although the present apocalyptic period is one of exceptional tensions, there is also at work an exceptional movement toward a compensating unity which refuses to violate the ultimate moral power at work in the universe, that very power upon which all human effort must at last depend. In this way we may come to understand that there exists an inherent interdependence of spiritual and mental growth which, though conditioned by circumstances, is never determined by circumstances. In this way the great plethora of human knowledge may be correlated with an insight into the nature of human nature by being attuned to the wide and deep range of human thought and human experience.

Incoherence is the result of the present disintegrative processes in education. Thus the need for *World Perspectives* expresses itself in the recognition that natural and man-made ecological systems require as much study as isolated particles of elementary reactions. For there is a basic correlation of elements in nature as in man which cannot be separated, which compose each other and alter each other mutually. Thus we hope to widen appropriately our conceptual framework of reference. For our epistemological problem consists in our finding the proper balance between our lack of an all-embracing principle relevant to our way of evaluating life and in our power to express ourselves in a logically consistent manner.

Our Judeo-Christian and Greco-Roman heritage, our Hellenic tradition, has compelled us to think in exclusive categories. But our *experience* challenges us to recognize a totality richer and far more complex than the average observer could have suspected—a totality which compels him to think in ways which the logic of dichotomies denies. We are summoned to revise fundamentally our ordinary ways of conceiving experience, and thus, by expanding our vision and by accepting those forms of thought which also include nonexclusive categories, the mind is then able to grasp what it was incapable of grasping or accepting before.

Nature operates out of necessity; there is no alternative in nature, no will, no freedom, no choice as there is for man. Man must have convictions and values to live for, and this also is recognized and accepted by those scientists who are at the same time philosophers. For they then realize that duty and devotion to our task, be it a task of acting or of understanding, will become weaker and rarer unless guidance is sought in a metaphysics that transcends our historical and scientific views or in a religion that transcends and yet pervades the work we are carrying on in the light of day.

For the nature of knowledge, whether scientific or ontological, consists in reconciling *meaning* and *being*. And *being* signifies nothing other than the actualization of potentiality, self-realization which keeps in tune with the transformation. This leads to experience in terms of the individual; and to organization and patterning in terms of the universe. Thus organism and world actualize themselves simultaneously.

And so we may conclude that organism is *being* enduring in time, in fact in eternal time, since it does not have its beginning with procreation, nor with birth, nor does it end with death. Energy and matter in whatever form they may manifest themselves are transtemporal and transspatial and are therefore metaphysical. Man as man is summoned to know what is right and what is wrong, for emptied of such knowledge he is unable to decide what is better or what is worse.

World Perspectives hopes to show that human society is different from animal societies, which, having reached a certain stage, are no longer progressive but are dominated by routine and repetition. Thus man has discovered his own nature, and with this self-knowledge he has left the state of nonage and entered manhood. For he is the only creature who is able to say not only "no" to life but "yes" and to make for himself a life that is human. In this decision lie his burden and his greatness. For the power of life or death lies not only in the tongue but in man's recently acquired ability to destroy or to create life itself, and therefore he is faced with unlimited and unprecedented choices for good and for evil that dominate our time. Our common concern is the very destiny of the human race. For man has now intervened in the process of evolution, a power not given to the pre-Socratics, nor to Aristotle, nor to the Prophets in the East or the West, nor to Copernicus, nor to Luther, Descartes, or Machiavelli. Judgments of value must henceforth direct technological change, for without such values man is divested of his humanity and of his need to collaborate with the very fabric of the universe in order to bestow meaning, purpose, and dignity upon his existence. No time must be lost since the wavelength of change is now shorter than the life-span of man.

In spite of the infinite obligation of men and in spite of their finite power, in spite of the intransigence of nationalisms, and in spite of the homelessness of moral passions rendered ineffectual by the technological outlook, beneath the apparent turmoil and upheaval of the present, and out of the transformations of this dynamic period with the unfolding of a world-consciousness, the purpose of *World Perspectives* is to help quicken the "unshaken heart of well-rounded truth" and interpret the significant elements of the World Age now taking shape out of the core of that undimmed continuity of the creative process which restores man to mankind while deepening and enhancing his communion and his symbiotic relationship with the universe.

RUTH NANDA ANSHEN

The Way to do is to be.

LAO-TSE

People should not consider so much what they are
to *do*, as what they *are*.

MASTER ECKHART

The less you *are* and the less you express of your
life—the more you *have* and the greater is your
alienated life.

KARL MARX

Foreword

This book follows two trends of my previous writings. First, it extends the development of my work in radical-humanistic psychoanalysis, concentrating on the analysis of selfishness and altruism as two basic character orientations. The last third of the book, Part Three, then carries further a theme I dealt with in *The Sane Society* and *The Revolution of Hope:* the crisis of contemporary society and possibilities for its solution. Repetitions of previously expressed thoughts have been unavoidable, but I hope the new viewpoint from which this small work is written and its extended concepts will compensate even readers who are familiar with my previous writings.

Actually, the title of this book and two earlier titles are almost identical: Gabriel Marcel, *Being and Having,* and Balthasar Staehelin, *Haben und Sein* (Having and Being). All three books are written in the spirit of humanism, but approach the subject in very different ways: Marcel writes from a theological and philosophical standpoint; Staehelin's book is a constructive discussion of materialism in modern science and a contribution to *Wirklichkeitsanalyse;* this volume deals with an empirical psychological and social analysis of the two modes of existence. I recommend the books by Marcel and Staehelin to readers who are sufficiently interested in the topic. (I did not know of the existence of a published English translation of Marcel's book until recently and read it instead in an excellent English translation prepared for my private use by Beverley Hughes. The published version is the one cited in the Bibliography.)

In the interest of making this a more readable book, its footnotes were reduced to a bare minimum, both in number and in length. While some book references appear in parentheses in the text, exact references are to be found in the Bibliography.

Another point of style that I want to clarify concerns the use of generic "man" and "he." I believe I have avoided all "male-oriented" language, and I thank Marion Odomirok for convincing me that the use of language in this respect is far more important than I used to think. On one point only have we been unable to agree in our approach to sexism in language, namely in respect to the world "man" as the term of reference for the species *Homo sapiens*. The use of "man" in this context, without differentiation of sex, has a long tradition in humanist thinking, and I do not believe we can do without a word that denotes clearly the human species character. No such difficulty exists in the German language: one uses the word *Mensch* to refer to the nonsex-differentiated being. But even in English the word "man" is used in the same sex-undifferentiated way as the German *Mensch*, as meaning human being or the human race. I think it is advisable to restore its nonsexual meaning to the word "man," rather than substituting awkward-sounding words. In this book I have capitalized "Man" in order to clarify my nonsex-differentiated use of the term.

There remains now only the pleasant task of expressing my thanks to the several persons who have contributed to the content and style of this book. First of all, I want to thank Rainer Funk, who was of great help to me in more than one respect: in long discussions he helped my understanding of fine points in Christian theology; he was untiring in pointing to literature in the field of theology; he read the manuscript several times and his excellent constructive suggestions as well as his critique helped greatly to enrich the manuscript and to eliminate some errors. I am most grateful to Marion Odomirok for greatly improving this book by her sensitive editing. My thanks also go to Joan Hughes, who conscientiously and patiently typed and retyped the numerous versions of the manuscript and made many excellent suggestions as to style and language. Finally, I thank Annis Fromm, who read the manuscript in its several versions and always responded with many valuable insights and suggestions.

E.F.

New York
June 1976

Introduction: The Great Promise, Its Failure, and New Alternatives

The End of an Illusion

The Great Promise of Unlimited Progress—the promise of domination of nature, of material abundance, of the greatest happiness for the greatest number, and of unimpeded personal freedom—has sustained the hopes and faith of the generations since the beginning of the industrial age. To be sure, our civilization began when the human race started taking active control of nature; but that control remained limited until the advent of the industrial age. With industrial progress, from the substitution of mechanical and then nuclear energy for animal and human energy to the substitution of the computer for the human mind, we could feel that we were on our way to unlimited production and, hence, unlimited consumption; that technique made us omnipotent; that science made us omniscient. We were on our way to becoming gods, supreme beings who could create a second world, using the natural world only as building blocks for our new creation.

Men and, increasingly, women experienced a new sense of freedom; they became masters of their own lives: feudal chains had been broken and one could do what one wished, free of all shackles. Or so people felt. And even though this was true only for the upper and middle classes, their achievement could lead others to the faith that eventually the new freedom could be extended to all members of society, provided industrialization kept up its pace. Socialism and communism quickly changed from a movement whose aim was a *new* society and a *new* man into one whose ideal was a bourgeois life for all, the *universalized bourgeois* as the men and women of the future. The achievement of wealth and comfort for all was supposed to result in unrestricted happiness for all. The trinity of unlimited production, absolute freedom, and unrestricted happiness formed the nucleus of a new religion, Progress, and a new Earthly City of Progress was to replace the City of God. It is not at all astonishing that this new religion provided its believers with energy, vitality, and hope.

The grandeur of the Great Promise, the marvelous material and intellectual achievements of the industrial age, must be visualized in order to understand the trauma that realization of its failure is producing today. For the industrial age has indeed failed to fulfill its Great Promise, and ever growing numbers of people are becoming aware that:

• Unrestricted satisfaction of all desires is not conducive to *well-being,* nor is it the way to happiness or even to maximum pleasure.

• The dream of being independent masters of our lives ended when we began awakening to the fact that we have all become cogs in the bureaucratic machine, with our thoughts, feelings, and tastes manipulated by government and industry and the mass communications that they control.

• Economic progress has remained restricted to the rich nations, and the gap between rich and poor nations has ever widened.

• Technical progress itself has created ecological dangers and the dangers of nuclear war, either or both of which may put an end to all civilization and possibly to all life.

When he came to Oslo to accept the Nobel Prize for Peace (1952), Albert Schweitzer challenged the world "to dare to face the situation. . . . Man has become a superman. . . . But the superman with the superhuman power has not risen to the level of superhuman reason. To the degree to which his power grows he becomes more and more a poor man. . . . It must shake up our conscience that we become all the more inhuman the more we grow into supermen."

Why Did the Great Promise Fail?

The failure of the Great Promise, aside from industrialism's essential economic contradictions, was built into the industrial system by its two main psychological premises: (1) that the aim of life is happiness, that is, maximum pleasure, defined as the satisfaction of any desire or subjective need a person may feel (*radical hedonism*); (2) that egotism, selfishness, and greed, as the system needs to generate them in order to function, lead to harmony and peace.

It is well known that the rich throughout history practiced radical hedonism. Those of unlimited means, such as the elite of Rome, of Italian cities of the Renaissance, and of England and France in the eighteenth and nineteenth centuries, tried to find a meaning to life in unlimited pleasure. But while maximum pleasure in the sense of radical hedonism was the practice of certain groups at certain times, with but a single exception prior to the seventeenth century, it was never the *theory* of well-being expressed by the great Masters of Living in China, India, the Near East, and Europe.

The one exception is the Greek philosopher Aristippus, a pupil of Socrates (first half of the fourth century B.C.), who taught that to experience an optimum of bodily pleasure is the goal of life and that happiness is the sum total of pleasures enjoyed. The little we know of his philosophy we owe to Diogenes Laertius, but it is enough to reveal Aristippus as the only real hedonist, for whom the existence of a desire is the basis for the right to satisfy it and thus to realize the goal of life: Pleasure.

Epicurus can hardly be regarded as representative of Aristippus' kind of hedonism. While for Epicurus "pure" pleasure is the highest goal, for him this pleasure meant "absence of pain" (*aponia*) and stillness of the soul (*ataraxia*). According to Epicurus, pleasure as satisfaction of a desire cannot be the aim of life, because such pleasure is necessarily followed by unpleasure and thus keeps humanity away from its real goal of absence of pain. (Epicurus' theory resembles Freud's in many ways.) Nevertheless, it seems that Epicurus represented a certain kind of subjectivism contrary to Aristotle's position, as far as the contradictory reports on Epicurus' statement permit a definite interpretation.

None of the other great Masters taught that the *factual existence of a desire constituted an ethical norm.* They were concerned with humankind's optimal well-being (*vivere bene*). The essential element in their thinking is the distinction between those needs (desires) that are only subjectively felt and whose satisfaction leads to momentary pleasure, and those needs that are rooted in human nature and whose realization is conducive to human growth and produces *eudaimonia,* i.e., "well-being." In other words, they were concerned with *the distinction between purely subjectively felt needs and objectively valid needs*—part of the former being harmful to human growth and the latter being in accordance with the requirements of human nature.

The theory that the aim of life is the fulfillment of every human desire was clearly voiced, for the first time since Aristippus, by philosophers in the seventeenth and eighteenth centuries. It was a concept that would easily arise when "profit" ceased to mean "profit for the soul" (as it does in the Bible and, even later, in Spinoza), but came to mean material, monetary profit, in the period when the middle class threw away not only its political shackles but also all bonds of love and solidarity and believed that being *only* for oneself meant being more rather than less oneself. For Hobbes happiness is the continuous progress from one greed (*cupiditas*) to another; La Mettrie even recommends drugs as giving at least the illusion of happiness; for de Sade the satisfaction of cruel impulses is legitimate, precisely because they exist and crave satisfaction. These were thinkers who lived in the age of the bourgeois class's final victory. What had been the unphilosophical practices of aristocrats became the practice and theory of the bourgeoisie.

Many ethical theories have been developed since the eighteenth century—some were more respectable forms of hedonism, such as Utilitarianism; others were strictly antihedonistic systems, such as those of Kant, Marx, Thoreau, and Schweitzer. Yet the present era, by and large since the end of the First World War, has returned to the practice and theory of radical hedonism. The concept of unlimited pleasure forms a strange contradiction to the ideal of disciplined work, similar to the contradiction between the acceptance of an obsessional work ethic and the ideal of complete laziness during the rest of the day and during vacations. The endless assembly line belt and the bureaucratic routine on the one hand, and television, the automobile, and sex on the other, make the contradictory combination possible. Obsessional work alone would drive people just as crazy as would complete laziness. With the combination, they can live. Besides, both contradictory attitudes correspond to an economic necessity: twentieth-century capitalism is based on maximal consumption of the goods and services produced as well as on routinized teamwork.

Theoretical considerations demonstrate that radical hedonism cannot lead to happiness as well as why it cannot do so, given human nature. But even without theoretical analysis the observable data show most clearly that our kind of "pursuit of happiness" does not produce well-being. We are a society of notoriously unhappy people: lonely, anxious, depressed, destructive, dependent—people who are glad when we have killed the time we are trying so hard to save.

Ours is the greatest social experiment ever made to solve the question whether pleasure (as a passive affect in contrast to the active affect, well-being and joy) can be a satisfactory answer to the problem of human existence. For the first time in history the satisfaction of the pleasure drive is not only the privilege of a minority but is possible for more than half the population. In the industrialized countries the experiment has already answered the question in the negative.

The second psychological premise of the industrial age, that the pursuit of individual egoism leads to harmony and peace, growth in everyone's welfare, is equally erroneous on theoretical grounds, and again its fallacy is proven by the observable data. Why should this principle, which only one of the great classical economists, David Ricardo, rejected, be true? To be an egoist refers not only to my behavior but to my character. It means: that I want everything for myself; that possessing, not sharing, gives me pleasure; that I must become greedy because if my aim is having, I *am* more the more I *have;* that I must feel antagonistic toward all others: my customers whom I want to deceive, my competitors whom I want to destroy, my workers whom I want to exploit. I can never be satisfied, because there is no end to my wishes; I must be envious of those who have more and afraid of those who have less. But I have to repress all these feelings in order to represent myself (to others as well as to myself) as the smiling, rational, sincere, kind human being everybody pretends to be.

The passion for having must lead to never-ending class war. The pretense of the communists that their system will end class struggle by abolishing classes is fiction, for their system is based on the principle of unlimited consumption as the goal of living. As long as everybody wants to have more, there must be formations of classes, there must be class war, and in global terms, there must be international war. *Greed and peace preclude each other*.

Radical hedonism and unlimited egotism could not have emerged as guiding principles of economic behavior had not a drastic change occurred in the eighteenth century. In medieval society, as in many other highly developed as well as primitive societies, economic behavior was determined by ethical principles. Thus, for the scholastic theologians, such economic categories as price and private property were part of moral theology. Granted that the theologians found formulations to adapt their moral code to the new economic demands (for instance Thomas Aquinas' qualification to the concept of "just price"); nevertheless, economic behavior remained *human* behavior and, hence, was subject to the values of humanistic ethics. Through a number of steps eighteenth-century capitalism underwent a radical change: economic behavior became separate from ethics and human values. Indeed, the economic machine was supposed to be an autonomous entity, independent of human needs and human will. It was a system that ran by itself and according to its own laws. The suffering of the workers as well as the destruction of an ever-increasing number of smaller enterprises for the sake of the growth of ever larger corporations was an economic necessity that one might regret, but that one had to accept as if it were the outcome of a natural law.

The development of this economic system was no longer determined by the question: *What is good for Man?* but by the question: *What is good for the growth of the system?* One tried to hide the sharpness of this conflict by making the assumption that what was good for the growth of the system (or even for a single big corporation) was also good for the people. This construction was bolstered by an auxiliary construction: that the very qualities that the system required of human beings—egotism, selfishness, and greed—were innate in human nature; hence, not only the system but human nature itself fostered them. Societies in which egotism, selfishness, and greed did not exist were supposed to be "primitive," their inhabitants "childlike." People refused to recognize that these traits were not natural drives that caused industrial society to exist, but that they were the *products* of social circumstances.

Not least in importance is another factor: people's relations to nature became deeply hostile. Being "freaks of nature" who by the very conditions of our existence are within nature and by the gift of our reason transcend it, we have tried to solve our existential problem by giving up the Messianic vision of harmony between humankind and nature by conquering nature, by transforming it to our own purposes until the conquest has become more and more equivalent to destruction. Our spirit of conquest and hostility has blinded us to the facts that natural resources have their limits and can eventually be exhausted, and that nature will fight back against human rapaciousness.

Industrial society has contempt for nature—as well as for all things not machine-made and for all people who are not machine makers (the nonwhite races, with the recent exceptions of Japan and China). People are attracted today to the mechanical, the powerful machine, the lifeless, and ever increasingly to destruction.

The Economic Necessity for Human Change

Thus far the argument here has been that the character traits engendered by our socioeconomic system, i.e., by our way of living, are pathogenic and eventually produce a sick person and, thus, a sick society. There is, however, a second argument from an entirely different viewpoint in favor of profound psychological changes in Man as an alternative to economic and ecological catastrophe. It is raised in two reports commissioned by the Club of Rome, one by D. H. Meadows et al., the other by M. D. Mesarovic and E. Pestel. Both reports deal with the technological, economic, and population trends on a world scale. Mesarovic and Pestel conclude that only drastic economic and technological changes on a global level, according to a master plan, can "avoid major and ultimately global catastrophe," and the data they array as proof of their thesis are based on the most global and systematic research that has been made so far. (Their book has certain methodological advantages over Meadows's report, but that earlier study considers even more drastic economic changes as an alternative to catastrophe.) Mesarovic and Pestel conclude, furthermore, that such economic changes are possible only *"if fundamental changes in the values and attitudes of man occur* [or as I would call it, in human character orientation], *such as a new ethic and a new attitude toward nature"* (emphasis added). What they are saying confirms only what others have said before and since their report was published, that a new society is possible *only if,* in the process of developing it, a new human being also develops, or in more modest terms, if a fundamental change occurs in contemporary Man's character structure.

Unfortunately, the two reports are written in the spirit of quantification, abstraction, and depersonalization so characteristic of our time, and besides that, they neglect completely all political and social factors, without which no realistic plan can possibly be made. Yet they present valuable data, and for the first time deal with the economic situation of the human race as a whole, its possibilities and its dangers. Their conclusion, that a new ethic and a new attitude toward nature are necessary, is all the more valuable because this demand is so contrary to their philosophical premises.

At the other end of the gamut stands E. F. Schumacher, who is also an economist, but at the same time a radical humanist. His demand for a radical human change is based on two arguments: that our present social order makes us sick, and that we are headed for an economic catastrophe unless we radically change our social system.

The need for profound human change emerges not only as an ethical or religious demand, not only as a psychological demand arising from the pathogenic nature of our present social character, but also as a condition for the sheer survival of the human race. Right living is no longer only the fulfillment of an ethical or religious demand. For the first time in history the *physical survival of the human race depends on a radical change of the human heart.* However, a change of the human heart is possible only to the extent that drastic economic and social changes occur that give the human heart the chance for change and the courage and the vision to achieve it.

Is There an Alternative to Catastrophe?

All the data mentioned so far are published and well known. The almost unbelievable fact is that no serious effort is made to avert what looks like a final decree of fate. While in our private life nobody except a mad person would remain passive in view of a threat to his total existence, those who are in charge of public affairs do practically nothing, and those who have entrusted their fate to them let them continue to do nothing.

How is it possible that the strongest of all instincts, that for survival, seems to have ceased to motivate us? One of the most obvious explanations is that the leaders undertake many actions that make it possible for them to pretend they are doing something effective to avoid a catastrophe: endless conferences, resolutions, disarmament talks, all give the impression that the problems are recognized and something is being done to resolve them. Yet nothing of real importance happens; but both the leaders and the led anesthetize their consciences and their wish for survival by giving the appearance of knowing the road and marching in the right direction.

Another explanation is that the selfishness the system generates makes leaders value personal success more highly than social responsibility. It is no longer shocking when political leaders and business executives make decisions that seem to be to their personal advantage, but at the same time are harmful and dangerous to the community. Indeed, if selfishness is one of the pillars of contemporary practical ethics, why should they act otherwise? They do not seem to know that greed (like submission) makes people stupid as far as the pursuit of even their own real interests is concerned, such as their interest in their own lives and in the lives of their spouses and their children (cf. J. Piaget, *The Moral Judgment of the Child*). At the same time, the general public is also so selfishly concerned with their private affairs that they pay little attention to all that transcends the personal realm.

Yet another explanation for the deadening of our survival instinct is that the changes in living that would be required are so drastic that people prefer the future catastrophe to the sacrifice they would have to make now. Arthur Koestler's description of an experience he had during the Spanish Civil War is a telling example of this widespread attitude: Koestler sat in the comfortable villa of a friend while the advance of Franco's troops was reported; there was no doubt that they would arrive during the night, and very likely he would be shot; he could save his life by fleeing, but the night was cold and rainy, the house, warm and cozy; so he stayed, was taken prisoner, and only by almost a miracle was his life saved many weeks later by the efforts of friendly journalists. This is also the kind of behavior that occurs in people who will risk dying rather than undergo an examination that could lead to the diagnosis of a grave illness requiring major surgery.

Aside from these explanations for fatal human passivity in matters of life and death, there is another, which is one of my reasons for writing this book. I refer to the view that we have no alternatives to the models of corporate capitalism, social democratic or Soviet socialism, or technocratic "fascism with a smiling face." The popularity of this view is largely due to the fact that little effort has been made to study the feasibility of entirely new social models and to experiment with them. Indeed, as long as the problems of social reconstruction will not, even if only partly, take the place of the preoccupation of our best minds with science and technique, the imagination will be lacking to visualize new and realistic alternatives.

The main thrust of this book is the analysis of the two basic modes of existence: the *mode of having* and the *mode of being*. In the opening chapter I present some "first glance" observations concerning the difference between the two modes. The second chapter demonstrates the difference, using a number of examples from daily experience that readers can easily relate to in their own personal experience. Chapter III presents the views on having and being in the Old and the New Testaments and in the writings of Master Eckhart. Subsequent chapters deal with the most difficult issue: the analysis of the difference between the having and the being modes of existence in which I attempt to build theoretical conclusions on the basis of the empirical data. While up to this point the book is mainly concerned with the individual aspects of the two basic modes of existence, the final chapters deal with the relevance of these modes in the formation of a New Man and a New Society and address themselves to the possibilities of alternatives to debilitating individual ill-being, and to catastrophic socioeconomic development of the whole world.

PART ONE

UNDERSTANDING THE DIFFERENCE BETWEEN HAVING AND BEING

I

A FIRST GLANCE

The Importance of the Difference
Between Having and Being

The alternative of *having* versus *being* does not appeal to
common sense. *To have,* so it would seem, is a normal
function of our life: in order to live we must have things.
Moreover, we must have things in order to enjoy them. In
a culture in which the supreme goal is to have—and to
have more and more—and in which one can speak of
someone as "being worth a million dollars," how can
there be an alternative between having and being? On the
contrary, it would seem that the very essence of being is
having; that if one *has* nothing, one *is* nothing.

Yet the great Masters of Living have made the alternative between having and being a central issue of their
respective systems. The Buddha teaches that in order to
arrive at the highest stage of human development, we
must not crave possessions. Jesus teaches: "For whosoever will save his life shall lose it; but whosoever will lose
his life for my sake, the same shall save it. For what is a
man advantaged, if he gain the whole world, and lose
himself, or be cast away?" (Luke 9:24-25). Master Eckhart taught that to have nothing and make oneself open
and "empty," not to let one's ego stand in one's way, is
the condition for achieving spiritual wealth and strength.
Marx taught that luxury is as much a vice as poverty
and that our goal should be to *be* much, not to *have*
much. (I refer here to the real Marx, the radical human-

3

ist, not to the vulgar forgery presented by Soviet communism.)

For many years I had been deeply impressed by this distinction and was seeking its empirical basis in the concrete study of individuals and groups by the psychoanalytic method. What I saw has led me to conclude that this distinction, together with that between love of life and love of the dead, represents the most crucial problem of existence; that empirical anthropological and psychoanalytic data tend to demonstrate that *having and being are two fundamental modes of experience, the respective strengths of which determine the differences between the characters of individuals and various types of social character.*

Examples in Various Poetic Expressions

As an introduction to understanding the difference between the having and being modes of existence, let me use as an illustration two poems of similar content that the late D.T. Suzuki referred to in "Lectures on Zen Buddhism." One is a haiku by a Japanese poet, Basho, 1644–1694; the other poem is by a nineteenth-century English poet, Tennyson. Each poet describes a similar experience: his reaction to a flower he sees while taking a walk. Tennyson's verse is:

> Flower in a crannied wall,
> I pluck you out of the crannies,
> I hold you here, root and all, in my hand,
> Little flower—but *if* I could understand
> What you are, root and all, and all in all,
> I should know what God and man is.

Translated into English, Basho's haiku runs something like this:

> When I look carefully
> I see the *nazuna* blooming
> By the hedge!

The difference is striking. Tennyson reacts to the flower by wanting to *have* it. He "plucks" it "root and all." And while he ends with an intellectual speculation about the flower's possible function for his attaining insight into the nature of God and man, the flower itself is killed as a result of his interest in it. Tennyson, as we see him in his poem, may be compared to the Western scientist who seeks the truth by means of dismembering life.

Basho's reaction to the flower is entirely different. He does not want to pluck it; he does not even touch it. All he does is "look carefully" to "see" it. Here is Suzuki's description:

It is likely that Basho was walking along a country road when he noticed something rather neglected by the hedge. He then approached closer, took a good look at it, and found it was no less than a wild plant, rather insignificant and generally unnoticed by passersby. This is a plain fact described in the poem with no specifically poetic feeling expressed anywhere except perhaps in the last two syllables, which read in Japanese *kana*. This particle, frequently attached to a noun or an adjective or an adverb, signifies a certain feeling of admiration or praise or sorrow or joy, and can sometimes quite appropriately be rendered into English by an exclamation mark. In the present *haiku* the whole verse ends with this mark.

Tennyson, it appears, needs to possess the flower in order to understand people and nature, and by his *having* it, the flower is destroyed. What Basho wants is to *see*, and not only to look at the flower, but to be at one, to "one" himself with it—and to let it live. The difference between Tennyson and Basho is fully explained in this poem by Goethe:

FOUND

I walked in the woods
All by myself,
To seek nothing,
That was on my mind.

I saw in the shade
A little flower stand,
Bright like the stars
Like beautiful eyes.

I wanted to pluck it,
But it said sweetly:
Is it to wilt
That I must be broken?

I took it out
With all its roots,
Carried it to the garden
At the pretty house.

And planted it again
In a quiet place;
Now it ever spreads
And blossoms forth.

Goethe, walking with no purpose in mind, is attracted by the brilliant little flower. He reports having the same impulse as Tennyson: to pluck it. But unlike Tennyson, Goethe is aware that this means killing the flower. For Goethe the flower is so much alive that it speaks and warns him; and he solves the problem differently from either Tennyson or Basho. He takes the flower "with all its roots" and plants it again so that its life is not destroyed. Goethe stands, as it were, between Tennyson and Basho: for him, at the crucial moment, the force of life is stronger than the force of mere intellectual curiosity. Needless to say that in this beautiful poem Goethe expresses the core of his concept of investigating nature.

Tennyson's relationship to the flower is in the mode of having, or possession—not material possession but the possession of knowledge. Basho's and Goethe's relationship to the flower each sees is in the mode of being. By being I refer to the mode of existence in which one neither *has* anything nor *craves to have* something, but is joyous, employs one's faculties productively, is *oned* to the world.

Goethe, the great lover of life, one of the outstanding fighters against human dismemberment and mechanization, has given expression to being as against having in many poems. His Faust is a dramatic description of the conflict between being and having (the latter represented by Mephistopheles), while in the following short poem he expresses the quality of being with the utmost simplicity:

PROPERTY

I know that nothing belongs to me
But the thought which unimpeded
From my soul will flow.
And every favorable moment
Which loving Fate
From the depth lets me enjoy.

The difference between being and having is not essentially that between East and West. The difference is rather between a society centered around persons and one centered around things. The having orientation is characteristic of Western industrial society, in which greed for money, fame, and power has become the dominant theme of life. Less alienated societies—such as medieval society, the Zuni Indians, the African tribal societies that were not affected by the ideas of modern "progress"—have their own Bashos. Perhaps after a few more generations of industrialization, the Japanese will have their Tennysons. It is not that Western Man cannot fully understand Eastern systems, such as Zen Buddhism (as Jung thought), but that modern man cannot understand the spirit of a society that is not centered in property and greed. Indeed, the writings of Master Eckhart (as difficult to understand as Basho or Zen) and the Buddha's writings are only two dialects of the same language.

Idiomatic Changes

A certain change in the emphasis on having and being is apparent in the growing use of nouns and the decreasing use of verbs in Western languages in the past few centuries.

A noun is the proper denotation for a thing. I can say

that I *have* things: for instance that I have a table, a house, a book, a car. The proper denotation for an activity, a process, is a verb: for instance I am, I love, I desire, I hate, etc. Yet ever more frequently an *activity* is expressed in terms of *having;* that is, a noun is used instead of a verb. But to express an activity by *to have* in connection with a noun is an erroneous use of language, because processes and activities cannot be possessed; they can only be experienced.

Older Observations: Du Marais—Marx

The evil consequences of this confusion were already recognized in the eighteenth century. Du Marais gave a very precise expression of the problem in his posthumously published work *Les Veritables Principles de la Grammarie* (1769). He writes: "In this example, *I have a watch, I have* must be understood in its proper sense; but in *I have an idea, I have* is said only by way of imitation. It is a borrowed expression. *I have an idea* means *I think, I conceive of in such and such a way. I have a longing* means *I desire; I have the will* means *I want,* etc." (my translation; I am indebted to Dr. Noam Chomsky for the reference to Du Marais).

A century after Du Marais observed this phenomenon of the substitution of nouns for verbs Marx and Engles deal with the same problem, but in a more radical fashion, in *The Holy Family.* Included in their critique of Edgar Bauer's "critical critique" is a small, but very important essay on love in which reference is made to the following statement by Bauer: "Love is a cruel goddess, who like all dieties, wants to possess the whole man and who is not content until he has sacrificed to her not only his soul but also his physical self. Her cult is suffering; the peak of this cult is self-sacrifice, is suicide" (my translation).

Marx and Engels answer: Bauer "transforms love into a 'goddess,' and into a 'cruel goddess' by transforming the *loving man* or the *love of man* into the *man of love;* he thus separates love as a separate being from man and makes it an independent entity" (my translation). Marx and Engels point here to a decisive factor in the use of the noun instead of the verb. The noun "love," which is only an abstraction for the activity of loving, becomes separated from the man. The loving man becomes the man of love. Love becomes a goddess, an idol into which the man projects his loving; in this process of alienation he ceases to experience love, but is in touch only with his capacity to love by his submission to the goddess Love. He has ceased to be an active person who feels; instead he has become an alienated worshiper of an idol.

Contemporary Usage

During the two hundred years since Du Marais, this trend of the substitution of nouns for verbs has grown to proportions that even he could hardly have imagined. Here is a typical, if slightly exaggerated, example of today's language. Assume that a person seeking a psychoanalyst's help opens the conversation with the following sentence: "Doctor, I *have* a problem; I *have* insomnia. Although I *have* a beautiful house, nice children, and a happy marriage, I *have* many worries." Some decades ago, instead of "I have a problem," the patient probably would have said, "I *am* troubled"; instead of "I *have* insomnia," "I *cannot* sleep"; instead of "I *have* a happy marriage," "I *am* happily married."

The more recent speech style indicates the prevailing high degree of alienation. By saying "I *have* a problem" instead of "I *am* troubled," subjective experience is eliminated: the *I* of experience is replaced by the *it* of possession. I have transformed my feeling into something I possess: the problem. But "problem" is an abstract expression for all kinds of difficulties. I cannot *have* a problem, because it is not a thing that can be owned; it, however, can have me. That is to say, I have transformed *myself* into "a problem" and am now owned by my creation. This way of speaking betrays a hidden, unconscious alienation.

Of course, one can argue that insomnia is a physical symptom like a sore throat or a toothache, and that it is therefore as legitimate to say that one *has* insomnia as it is to say that one *has* a sore throat. Yet there is a difference: a sore throat or a toothache is a bodily sensation that can be more or less intense, but it has little psychical quality. One can *have* a sore throat, for one has a throat, or an aching tooth, for one has teeth. Insomnia, on the contrary, is not a bodily sensation but a state of mind, that of not being able to sleep. If I speak of "having insomnia" instead of saying "I cannot sleep," I betray my wish to push away the experience of anxiety, restlessness, tension that prevents me from sleeping, and to deal with the mental phenomenon *as if it were* a bodily symptom.

For another example: To say, "I have great love for you," is meaningless. Love is not a thing that one can have, but a *process*, an inner activity that one is the subject of. I can love, I can *be* in love, but in loving, I *have* ... nothing. In fact, the less I have, the more I can love.

Origin of the Terms

"To have" is a deceptively simple expression. Every human being *has* something: a body,* clothes, shelter— on up to the modern man or woman who has a car, a television set, a washing machine, etc. Living without having something is virtually impossible. Why, then, should having be a problem? Yet the linguistic history of "having" indicates that the word is indeed a problem. To those who believe that to have is a most natural category of human existence it may come as a surprise to learn that many languages have no word for "to have." In Hebrew, for instance, "I have" must be expressed by the indirect form *jesh li* ("it is to me"). In fact, languages that express possession in this way, rather than by "I have," predominate. It is interesting to note that in the development of many languages the construction "it is to

---

*It should be mentioned here, at least in passing, that there also exists a being relationship to one's body that experiences the body as alive, and that can be expressed by saying "I am my body," rather than "I have my body"; all practices of sensory awareness attempt this being experience of the body.

me" is followed later on by the construction "I have," but as Emile Benveniste has pointed out, the evolution does not occur in the reverse direction.* This fact suggests that the word for *to have* develops in connection with the development of private property, while it is absent in societies with predominantly functional property, that is, possession for use. Further sociolinguistic studies should be able to show if and to what extent this hypothesis is valid.

If *having* seems to be a relatively simple concept, *being*, or the form "to be," is all the more complicated and difficult. "Being" is used in several different ways: (1) as a copula—such as "I am tall," "I am white," "I am poor," i.e., a grammatical denotation of identity (many languages do not have a word for "to be" in this sense; Spanish distinguishes between permanent qualities, *ser*, which belong to the essence of the subject, and contingent qualities, *estar*, which are not of the essence); (2) as the passive, suffering form of a verb—for example, "I am beaten" means I am the object of another's activity, not the subject of my activity, as in "I beat"; (3) as meaning to exist—wherein, as Beneveniste has shown, the "to be" of existence is a different term from "to be" as a copula stating identity: "The two words have coexisted and can still coexist, although they are entirely different."

Benveniste's study throws new light on the meaning of "to be" as a verb in its own right rather than as a copula. "To be," in Indo-European languages, is expressed by the root *es*, the meaning of which is "to have existence, to be found in reality." Existence and reality are defined as "that which is authentic, consistent, "true." (In Sanskrit, *sant*, "existent," "actual good," "true"; superlative *Sattama*, "the best.") "Being" in its etymological root is thus more than a statement of identity between subject and attribute; it is more than a *descriptive* term for a phenomenon. It denotes the reality of existence of who or what *is*; it states his/her/its authenticity and truth. Stating that

---

*This and the following linguistic quotations are taken from Benveniste.

somebody or something *is* refers to the person's or the thing's essence, not to his/her/its appearance.

This preliminary survey of the meaning of having and being leads to these conclusions:

1. By being or having I do not refer to certain separate qualities of a subject as illustrated in such statements as "I have a car" or "I am white" or "I am happy." I refer to two fundamental modes of existence, to two different kinds of orientation toward self and the world, to two different kinds of character structure the respective predominance of which determines the totality of a person's thinking, feeling, and acting.

2. In the having mode of existence my relationship to the world is one of possessing and owning, one in which I want to make everybody and everything, including myself, my property.

3. In the being mode of existence, we must identify two forms of being. One is in contrast to *having,* as exemplified in the Du Marais statement, and means aliveness and authentic relatedness to the world. The other form of being is in contrast to *appearing* and refers to the true nature, the true reality, of a person or a thing in contrast to deceptive appearances as exemplified in the etymology of being (Benveniste).

Philosophical Concepts of Being

The discussion of the concept of being is additionally complicated because being has been the subject matter of many thousands of philosophical books and "What is being?" has been one of the crucial questions of Western philosophy. While the concept of being will be treated here from anthropological and psychological points of view, the philosophical discussion is, of course, not unrelated to the anthropological problems. Since even a brief presentation of the development of the concept of being in the history of philosophy from the pre-Socratics to modern philosophy would go beyond the given limits of this book, I shall mention only one crucial point: the concept of *process, activity, and movement as an element in being*. As George Simmel has pointed out, the idea that being implies change, i.e., that being is *becoming*, has its two greatest and most uncompromising representatives at the beginning and at the zenith of Western philosophy: in Heraclitus and in Hegel.

The position that being is a permanent, timeless, and unchangeable substance and the opposite of becoming, as expressed by Parmenides, Plato, and the scholastic "realists," makes sense only on the basis of the idealistic notion that a thought (idea) is the ultimate reality. If the *idea* of love (in Plato's sense) is more real than the experience of loving, one can say that love as an idea is permanent and unchangeable. But when we start out with the reality of human beings existing, loving, hating, suffering, then there is no being that is not at the same time becoming and changing. Living structures can be only if they become; they can exist only if they change. Change and growth are inherent qualities of the life process.

Heraclitus' and Hegel's radical concept of life as a process and not as a substance is paralleled in the Eastern world by the philosophy of the Buddha. There is no room in Buddhist thought for the concept of any enduring permanent substance, neither things nor the self. Nothing is real but processes.* Contemporary scientific thought has brought about a renaissance of the philosophical concepts of "process thinking" by discovering and applying them to the natural sciences.

Having and Consuming

Before discussing some simple illustrations of the having and being modes of existence, another manifestation of having must be mentioned, that of *incorporating*. Incorporating a thing, for instance by eating or drinking, is

---

*Z. Fišer, one of the most outstanding, though little-known, Czech philosophers, has related the Buddhist concept of process to authentic Marxian philosophy. Unfortunately, the work has been published only in the Czech language and hence has been inaccessible to most Western readers. (I know it from a private English translation.)

an archaic form of possessing it. At a certain point in its development an infant tends to take things it wants into its mouth. This is the infant's form of taking possession, when its bodily development does not yet enable it to have other forms of controlling its possessions. We find the same connection between incorporation and possession in many forms of cannibalism. For example: by eating another human being, I acquire that person's powers (thus cannibalism can be the magic equivalent of acquiring slaves); by eating the heart of a brave man, I acquire his courage; by eating a totem animal, I acquire the divine substance the totem animal symbolizes.

Of course, most objects cannot be incorporated physically (and inasmuch as they could, they would be lost again in the process of elimination). But there is also *symbolic* and *magic* incorporation. If I believe I have incorporated a god's, a father's, or an animal's image, it can neither be taken away nor eliminated. I swallow the object symbolically and believe in its symbolic presence within myself. This is, for instance, how Freud explained the superego: the introjected sum total of the father's prohibitions and commands. An authority, an institution, an idea, an image can be introjected in the same way: I *have* them, eternally protected in my bowels, as it were. ("Introjection" and "identification" are often used synonymously, but it is difficult to decide whether they are really the same process. At any rate, "identification" should not be used loosely, when one should better talk of imitation or subordination.)

There are many other forms of incorporation that are not connected with physiological needs and, hence, are not limited. The attitude inherent in consumerism is that of swallowing the whole world. The consumer is the eternal suckling crying for the bottle. This is obvious in pathological phenomena, such as alcoholism and drug addiction. We apparently single out both these addictions because their effects interfere with the addicted person's social obligations. Compulsive smoking is not thus censured because, while not less of an addiction, it does not interfere with the smokers' social functions, but possibly "only" with their life spans.

Further attention is given to the many forms of everyday consumerism later on in this volume. I might only remark here that as far as leisure time is concerned, automobiles, television, travel, and sex are the main objects of present-day consumerism, and while we speak of them as leisure-time activities, we would do better to call them leisure-time *passivities*.

To sum up, to consume is one form of having, and perhaps the most important one for today's affluent industrial societies. Consuming has ambiguous qualities: It relieves anxiety, because what one has cannot be taken away; but it also requires one to consume ever more, because previous consumption soon loses its satisfactory character. Modern consumers may identify themselves by the formula: I *am* = *what I have and what I consume*.

II

HAVING AND BEING IN DAILY EXPERIENCE

Because the society we live in is devoted to acquiring property and making a profit, we rarely see any evidence of the being mode of existence and most people see the having mode as the most natural mode of existence, even the only acceptable way of life. All of which makes it especially difficult for people to comprehend the nature of the being mode, and even to understand that having is only one possible orientation. Nevertheless, these two concepts are rooted in human experience. Neither one should be, or can be, examined in an abstract, purely cerebral way; both are reflected in our daily life and must be dealt with concretely. The following simple examples of how having and being are demonstrated in everyday life may help readers to understand these two alternative modes of existence

Learning

Students in the having mode of existence will listen to a lecture, hearing the words and understanding their logical structure and their meaning and, as best they can, will write down every word in their looseleaf notebooks—so that, later on, they can memorize their notes and thus pass an examination. But the content does not become part of their own individual system of thought, enriching and widening it. Instead, they transform the words they hear into fixed clusters of thought, or whole theories, which they store up. The students and the content of the lectures remain strangers to each other, except that each student has become the owner of a collection of statements made by somebody else (who had either created them or taken them over from another source).

Students in the having mode have but one aim: to hold onto what they "learned," either by entrusting it firmly to their memories or by carefully guarding their notes. They do not have to produce or create something new. In fact, the *having*-type individuals feel rather disturbed by new thoughts or ideas about a subject, because the new puts into question the fixed sum of information they have. Indeed, to one for whom having is the main form of relatedness to the world, ideas that cannot easily be pinned down (or penned down) are frightening—like everything else that grows and changes, and thus is not controllable.

The process of learning has an entirely different quality for students in the being mode of relatedness *to* the world. To begin with, they do not go to the course of lectures, even to the first one in a course, as *tabulae rasae*. They have thought beforehand about the problems the lectures will be dealing with and have in mind certain questions and problems of their own. They have been occupied with the topic and it interests them. Instead of being passive receptacles of words and ideas, they listen, they *hear,* and most important, they *receive* and they *respond* in an active, productive way. What they listen to stimulates their own thinking processes. New questions, new ideas, new perspectives arise in their minds. Their listening is an alive process. They listen with interest, hear what the lecturer says, and spontaneously come to life in response to what they hear. They do not simply acquire knowledge that they can take home and memorize. Each student has been affected and has changed: each is different after the lecture than he or she was before it. Of course, this mode of learning can prevail only if the lecture offers stimulating material. Empty talk cannot be responded to in the being mode, and in such circumstances, students in the being mode find it best not to listen at all, but to concentrate on their own thought processes.

At least a passing reference should be made here to the word "interests," which in current usage has become a pallid, worn-out expression. Yet its essential meaning is contained in its root: Latin, *inter-esse*, "to be in [or] among" it. This active interest was expressed in Middle English by the term "to list" (adjective, listy; adverb, listily). In modern English, "to list" is only used in a spatial sense: "a ship lists"; the original meaning in a psychical sense we have only in the negative "listless." "To list" once meant "to be actively striving for," "to be genuinely interested in." The root is the same as that of "lust," but "to list" is not a lust one is *driven by,* but the *free and active interest in, or striving for.* "To list" is one of the key expressions of the anonymous author (mid-fourteenth century) of *The Cloud of Unknowing* (Evelyn Underhill, ed.). That the language has retained the word only in its negative sense is characteristic of the change of spirit in society from the thirteenth to the twentieth century.

Remembering

Remembering can occur in either the having or the being mode. What matters most for the difference between the two forms of remembering is the *kind* of connection that is made. In the having mode of remembering, the connection is entirely *mechanical,* as when the connection between one word and the next becomes firmly established by the frequency with which it is made. Or the connections may be purely *logical,* such as the connection between opposites, or between converging concepts, or with time, space, size, color, or within a given system of thought.

In the being mode, remembering is *actively* recalling words, ideas, sights, paintings, music; that is, connecting the single datum to be remembered and the many other data that it is connected with. The connections in the case of being are neither mechanical nor purely logical, but alive. One concept is connected with another by a productive act of thinking (or feeling) that is mobilized when one searches for the right word. A simple example: If I associate the word "headache" with the word "aspirin," I form a logical, conventional association. But if I associate the word "headache" with "stress" or "anger," I connect the given datum with its possible causes, an insight I have arrived at in studying the phenomenon. This latter type of remembering constitutes in itself an act of productive thinking. The most striking examples of this kind of alive remembering are the "free associations" devised by Freud.

Persons not mainly inclined toward storing up data will find that their memories, in order to function well, need a strong and immediate *interest*. For example, individuals have been known to remember words of a long-forgotten foreign language when it has been of vital importance to do so. And in my own experience, while I am not endowed with a particularly good memory, I have remembered the dream of a person I analyzed, be it two weeks or five years ago, when I again come face to face with and concentrate on the whole personality of that person. Yet not five minutes before, in the cold as it were, I was quite unable to remember that dream.

Remembering in the mode of being implies bringing to life something one saw or heard before. We can experience this productive remembering by trying to envision a person's face or scenery that we had once seen. We will not be able to remember instantly in either case; we must re-create the subject, bring it to life in our mind. This kind of remembering is not always easy; to be able to fully recall the face or the scenery one must once have seen it with sufficient concentration. When such remembering is fully achieved, the person whose face is recalled is as alive, the remembered scenery as vivid, as if that person or that scenery were actually physically before one.

The way those in the having mode remember a face or scenery is typified by the way most people look at a photograph. The photograph serves only as an aid to their memory in identifying a person or a scene, and the usual reaction it elicits is: "Yes, that's him"; or "Yes, I've been there." The photograph becomes, for most people, an *alienated* memory.

Memory entrusted to paper is another form of alienated remembering. By writing down what I want to remember I am sure to *have* that information, and I do not try to engrave it on my brain. I am sure of my possession—except that when I have lost my notes, I have lost my memory of the information, too. My capacity to remember has left me, for my memory bank had become an externalized part of me, in the form of my notes.

Considering the multitude of data that people in contemporary society need to remember, a certain amount of notemaking and information deposited in books is unavoidable. One can easily and best observe in oneself that writing down things diminishes one's power of remembering, but some typical examples may prove helpful.

An everyday example occurs in stores. Today a salesclerk will rarely do a simple addition of two or three items in his or her head, but will immediately use a machine. The classroom provides another example. Teachers can observe that the students who carefully write down every sentence of the lecture will, in all likelihood, understand and remember less than the students who trusted their capacity to understand and, hence, remember at least the essentials. Further, musicians know that those who most easily sight-read a score have more difficulty in remembering the music without the score.* (Toscanini, whose memory was known to be extraordinary, is a good example of a musician in the being mode.) For a final example, in Mexico I have observed that people who are illiterate or who write little have memories far superior to the fluently literate inhabitants of the industrialized countries. Among other facts, this suggests that literacy is by no means the blessing it is advertised to be, especially when people use it merely to read material that impoverishes their capacity to experience and to imagine.

---

*This information was provided by Dr. Moshe Budmor.

Conversing

The difference between the having and being modes can be easily observed in two examples of conversations. Let us take a typical conversational debate between two men in which A *has* opinion X and B *has* opinion Y. Each identifies with his own opinion. What matters to each is to find better, i.e., more reasonable, arguments to defend his opinion. Neither expects to change his own opinion, or that his opponent's opinion will change. Each is afraid of changing his own opinion, precisely because it is one of his possessions, and hence its loss would mean an impoverishment.

The situation is somewhat different in a conversation that is not meant to be a debate. Who has not experienced meeting a person distinguished by prominence or fame or even by real qualities, or a person of whom one wants something: a good job, to be loved, to be admired? In any such circumstances many people tend to be at last mildly anxious, and often they "prepare" themselves for the important meeting. They think of topics that might interest the other; they think in advance how they might begin the conversation; some even map out the whole conversation, as far as their own part is concerned. Or they may bolster themselves up by thinking about what they *have*: their past successes, their charming personality (or their intimidating personality if this role is more effective), their social position, their connections, their appearance and dress. In a word, they mentally balance their worth, and based on this evaluation, they display their wares in the ensuing conversation. The person who is very good at this will indeed impress many people, although the created impression is only partly due to the individual's performance and largely due to the poverty of most people's judgment. If the performer is not so clever, however, the performance will appear wooden, contrived, boring and will not elicit much interest.

In contrast are those who approach a situation by preparing nothing in advance, not bolstering themselves up in any way. Instead, they respond spontaneously and productively; they forget about themselves, about the knowledge, the positions they have. Their egos do not stand in their own way, and it is precisely for this reason that they can fully respond to the other person and that person's ideas. They give birth to new ideas, because they are not holding onto anything. While the having persons rely on what they *have,* the being persons rely on the fact that they *are,* that they are alive and that something new will be born if only they have the courage to let go and to respond. They come fully alive in the conversation, because they do not stifle themselves by anxious concern with what they have. Their own aliveness is infectious and often helps the other person to transcend his or her egocentricity. Thus the conversation ceases to be an exchange of commodities (information, knowledge, status) and becomes a dialogue in which it does not matter any more who is right. The duelists begin to dance together, and they part not with triumph or sorrow—which are equally sterile—but with joy. (The essential factor in psychoanalytic therapy is this enlivening quality of the therapist. No amount of psychoanalytic interpretation will have an effect if the therapeutic atmosphere is heavy, unalive, and boring.)

Reading

What holds true for a conversation holds equally true for reading, which is—or should be—a conversation between the author and the reader. Of course, in reading (as well as in a personal conversation) *whom* I read from (or talk with) is important. Reading an artless, cheap novel is a form of day-dreaming. It does not permit productive response; the text is swallowed like a television show, or the potato chips one munches while watching TV. But a novel, say by Balzac, can be read with inner participation, productively—that is, in the mode of being. Yet probably most of the time it is also read in the mode of consuming—of having. Their curiosity having been aroused, the readers want to know the plot: whether the hero dies or lives, whether the heroine is seduced or resists; they want to know the answers. The novel serves as a kind of foreplay to excite them; the happy or unhappy end culminates their experience: when they know the end, they *have* the whole story, almost as real as if they rummaged in their own memories. But they have not enhanced their knowledge; they have not understood the person in the novel and thus have not deepened their insight into human nature, or gained knowledge about themselves.

The modes of reading are the same with regard to a book whose theme is philosophy or history. The way one reads a philosophy or history book is formed—or better, deformed—by education. The school aims to give each student a certain amount of "cultural property," and at the end of their schooling certifies the students as *having* at least the minimum amount. Students are taught to read a book so that they can repeat the author's main thoughts. This is how the students "know" Plato, Aristotle, Descartes, Spinoza, Leibniz, Kant, Heidegger, Sartre. The difference between various levels of education from high school to graduate school is mainly in the amount of cultural property that is acquired, which corresponds roughly to the amount of material property the students may be expected to own in later life. The so-called excellent students are the ones who can most accurately repeat what each of the various philosophers had to say. They are like a well-informed guide at a museum. What they do not learn is that which goes beyond this kind of property knowledge. They do not learn to question the philosophers, to talk to them; they do not learn to be aware of the philosophers' own contradictions, of their leaving out certain problems or evading issues; they do not learn to distinguish between what was new and what the authors could not help thinking because it was the "common sense" of their time; they do not learn to hear so that they are able to distinguish when the authors speak only from their brain and when their brain and heart speak together; they do not learn to discover whether the authors are authentic or fake; and many more things.

The mode of being readers will often come to the

conclusion that even a highly praised book is entirely without or of very limited value. Or they may have fully understood a book, sometimes better than had the author, who may have considered everything he or she wrote as being equally important.

Exercising Authority

Another example of the difference between the modes of having and being is the exercise of authority. The crucial point is expressed in the difference between *having* authority and *being* an authority. Almost all of us exercise authority at least at some stage of our lives. Those who bring up children must exercise authority—whether they want to or not—in order to protect their children from dangers and give them at least minimal advice on how to act in various situations. In a patriarchal society women, too, are objects of authority, for most men. Most members of a bureaucratic, hierarchically organized society like ours exercise authority, except the people on the lowest social level, who are only objects of authority.

Our understanding of authority in the two modes depends on our recognizing that "authority" is a broad term with two entirely different meanings: it can be either "rational" or "irrational" authority. Rational authority is based on competence, and it helps the person who leans on it to grow. Irrational authority is based on power and serves to exploit the person subjected to it. (I have discussed this distinction in *Escape from Freedom*.)

Among the most primitive societies, i.e., the hunters and food gatherers, authority is exercised by the person who is generally recognized as being competent for the task. What qualities this competence rests on depends much on the specific circumstances; generally they would include experience, wisdom, generosity, skill, "presence," courage. No permanent authority exists in many of these tribes, but an authority emerges in the case of need. Or there are different authorities for different occasions: war, religious practice, adjustment of quarrels. When the qualities on which the authority rests disappear or weaken, the authority itself ends. A very similar form of authority may be observed among many primate societies, in which competence is often established not by physical strength but by such qualities as experience and "wisdom." In a very ingenious experiment with monkeys, J. M. R. Delgado (1967) has shown that if the dominant animal even momentarily loses the qualities that constitute its competence, its authority ends.

Being-authority is grounded not only in the individual's competence to fulfill certain social functions, but equally so in the very essence of a personality that has achieved a high degree of growth and integration. Such persons radiate authority and do not have to give orders, threaten, bribe. They are highly developed individuals who demonstrate by what they are—and not mainly by what they do or say—what human beings can be. The great Masters of Living were such authorities, and to a lesser degree of perfection, such individuals may be found on all educational levels and in the most diverse cultures. (The problem of education hinges on this point. If parents were more developed themselves and rested in their own center, the opposition between authoritarian and laissez-faire education would hardly exist. Needing this being-authority, the child reacts to it with great eagerness; on the other hand, the child rebels against pressure or neglect by people who show by their own behavior that they themselves have not made the effort they expect from the growing child.)

With the formation of societies based on a hierarchical order and much larger and more complex than those of the hunters and food gatherers, authority by competence yields to authority by social status. This does not mean that the existing authority is necessarily incompetent; it does mean that competence is not an essential element of authority. Whether we deal with monarchical authority—where the lottery of genes decides qualities of competence—or with an unscrupulous criminal who succeeds in becoming an authority by murder or treachery, or, as frequently in modern democracy, with authorities elected on the basis of their photogenic physiognomy or the amount of money they can spend on their election, in all these cases there may be almost no relation between competence and authority.

But there are even serious problems in the cases of authority established on the basis of some competence: a leader may have been competent in one field, incompetent in another—for instance, a statesman may be competent in conducting war and incompetent in the situation of peace; or a leader who is honest and courageous at the beginning of his or her career loses these qualities by the seduction of power; or age or physical troubles may lead to a certain deterioration. Finally, one must consider that it is much easier for the members of a small tribe to judge the behavior of an authority than it is for the millions of people in our system, who know their candidate only by the artificial image created by public relations specialists.

Whatever the reasons for the loss of the competence-forming qualities, in most larger and hierarchically organized societies the process of alienation of authority occurs. The real or alleged initial competence is transferred to the uniform or to the title of the authority. If the authority wears the proper uniform or has the proper title, this external sign of competence replaces the real competence and its qualities. The king—to use this title as a symbol for this type of authority—can be stupid, vicious, evil, i.e., utterly incompetent to *be* an authority, yet he *has* authority. As long as he has the title, he is supposed to have the qualities of competence. Even if the emperor is naked, everybody believes he wears beautiful clothes.

That people take uniforms and titles for the real qualities of competence is not something that happens quite of itself. Those who have these symbols of authority and those who benefit therefrom must dull their subject people's realistic, i.e., critical, thinking and make them believe the fiction. Anybody who will think about it knows the machinations of propaganda, the methods by which critical judgment is destroyed, how the mind is lulled into submission by clichés, how people are made dumb because they become dependent and lose their capacity to trust their eyes and judgment. They are blinded to reality by the fiction they believe.

Having Knowledge and Knowing

The difference between the mode of having and the mode of being in the sphere of *knowing* is expressed in two formulations: "I have knowledge" and "I know." *Having* knowledge is taking and keeping possession of available knowledge (information); *knowing* is functional and part of the process of productive thinking.

Our understanding of the quality of knowing in the being mode of existence can be enhanced by the insights of such thinkers as the Buddha, the Hebrew prophets, Jesus, Master Eckhart, Sigmund Freud, and Karl Marx. In their view, knowing begins with the awareness of the deceptiveness of our common sense perceptions, in the sense that our picture of physical reality does not correspond to what is "really real" and, mainly, in the sense that most people are half-awake, half-dreaming, and are unaware that most of what they hold to be true and self-evident is illusion produced by the suggestive influence of the social world in which they live. Knowing, then, begins with the shattering of illusions, with *dis*illusionment (*Ent-täuschung*). Knowing means to penetrate through the surface, in order to arrive at the roots, and hence the causes; knowing means to "see" reality in its nakedness. Knowing does not mean to be in possession of the truth; it means to penetrate the surface and to strive critically and actively in order to approach truth ever more closely.

This quality of creative penetration is expressed in the Hebrew *jadoa,* which means to know and to love, in the sense of male sexual penetration. The Buddha, the Awakened One, calls on people to wake up and liberate themselves from the illusion that craving for things leads to happiness. The Hebrew prophets appeal to the people to wake up and know that their idols are nothing but the work of their own hands, are illusions. Jesus says: "The truth shall make you free!" Master Eckhart expressed his concept of knowing many times; for instance, when speaking of God he says: "Knowledge is no particular thought but rather it peels off [all coverings] and is disinterested and runs naked to God, until it touches him and grasps him" (Blakney, p. 243). ("Nakedness" and "naked" are favorite expressions of Master Eckhart as well as of his contemporary, the anonymous author of *The Cloud of Unknowing.*) According to Marx, one needs to destroy illusions in order to create the conditions that make illusions unnecessary. Freud's concept of self-knowledge is based on the idea of destroying illusions ("rationalizations") in order to become aware of the unconscious reality. (The last of the Enlightenment thinkers, Freud can be called a revolutionary thinker in terms of the eighteenth-century Enlightenment philosophy, not in terms of the twentieth century.)

All these thinkers were concerned with human salvation; they were all critical of socially accepted thought patterns. To them the aim of knowing is not the certainty of "absolute truth," something one can feel secure with, but *the self-affirming process of human reason.* Ignorance, for the one who *knows,* is as good as knowledge, since both are part of the process of knowing, even though ignorance of this kind is different from the ignorance of the unthinking. Optimum knowledge in the being mode is *to know more deeply.* In the having mode it is *to have more knowledge.*

Our education generally tries to train people to *have* knowledge as a possession, by and large commensurate with the amount of property or social prestige they are likely to have in later life. The minimum they receive is the amount they will need in order to function properly in their work. In addition they are each given a "luxury-knowledge package" to enhance their feeling of worth, the size of each such package being in accord with the person's probable social prestige. The schools are the factories in which these overall knowledge packages are produced—although schools usually claim they mean to bring the students in touch with the highest achievements of the human mind. Many undergraduate colleges are particularly adroit in nurturing these illusions. From Indian thought and art to existentialism and surrealism, a vast smörgåsbord of knowledge is offered from which students pick a little here, a little there, and in the name

of spontaneity and freedom are not urged to concentrate
on one subject, not even ever to finish reading an entire
book. (Ivan Illich's radical critique of the school system
brings many of its failings into focus.)

Faith

In a religious, political, or personal sense the concept
of faith can have two entirely different meanings, depending upon whether it is used in the having mode or in the
being mode.

Faith, in the having mode, is the possession of an
answer for which one has no rational proof. It consists of
formulations created by others, which one accepts because one submits to those others—usually a bureaucracy. It carries the feeling of certainty because of the real
(or only imagined) power of the bureaucracy. It is the
entry ticket to join a large group of people. It relieves one
of the hard task of thinking for oneself and making decisions. One becomes one of the *beati possidentes,* the happy owners of the right faith. Faith, in the having mode,
gives certainty; it claims to pronounce ultimate, unshak-
able knowledge, which is believable because the power of
those who promulgate and protect the faith seems un-
shakable. Indeed, who would not choose certainty, if all it
requires is to surrender one's independence?

God, originally a symbol for the highest value that we
can experience within us, becomes, in the having mode,
an idol. In the prophetic concept, an idol is a *thing* that
we ourselves make and project our own powers into, thus
impoverishing ourselves. We then submit to our creation
and by our submission are in touch with ourselves in an
alienated form. While I can *have* the idol because it is a
thing, by my submission to it, *it,* simultaneously, has *me.*
Once He has become an idol, God's alleged qualities have
as little to do with my personal experience as alienated
political doctrines do. The idol may be praised as Lord of
Mercy, yet any cruelty may be committed in its name,
just as the alienated faith in human solidarity may not
even raise doubts about committing the most inhuman
acts. Faith, in the having mode, is a crutch for those who

want to be certain, those who want an answer to life without daring to search for it themselves.

In the being mode, faith is an entirely different phenomenon. Can we live without faith? Must not the nursling have faith in its mother's breast? Must we all not have faith in other beings, in those whom we love, and in ourselves? Can we live without faith in the validity of norms for our life? Indeed, without faith we become sterile, hopeless, afraid to the very core of our being.

Faith, in the being mode, is not, in the first place, a belief in certain ideas (although it may be that, too) but an inner orientation, an *attitude*. It would be better to say that one *is in* faith than that one *has* faith. (The theological distinction between faith that *is* belief [*fides quae creditur*] and faith *as* belief [*fides qua creditur*] reflects a similar distinction between the *content* of faith and the *act* of faith.) One can be in faith toward oneself and toward others, and the religious person can be in faith toward God. The God of the Old Testament is, first of all, a negation of idols, of gods whom one can *have*. Though conceived in analogy to an Oriental king, the concept of God transcends itself from the very beginning. God must not have a name; no image must be made of God.

Later on, in Jewish and Christian development, the attempt is made to achieve the complete deidolization of God, or rather to fight the danger of idolization by postulating that not even God's qualities can be stated. Or most radically in Christian mysticism—from (Pseudo) Dionysius Areopagita to the unknown author of *The Cloud of Unknowing* and to Master Eckhart—the concept of God tends to be that of the One, the "Godhead" (the No-thing), thus joining views expressed in the Vedas and in Neoplatonic thinking. This faith in God is vouched for by inner experience of the divine qualities in oneself; it is a continuous, active process of self-creation—or, as Master Eckhart puts it, of Christ's eternally being born within ourselves.

My faith in myself, in another, in humankind, in our capacity to become fully human also implies certainty, but certainty based on my own experience and not on my submission to an authority that dictates a certain belief. It is certainty of a truth that cannot be proven by rationally compelling evidence, yet truth I am certain of because of my experiential, subjective evidence. (The Hebrew word for faith is *emunah,* "certainty"; *amen* means "certainly.")

If I am certain of a man's integrity, I could not prove his integrity up to his last day; strictly speaking, if his integrity remains inviolate to the time of his death, even that would not exclude a positivistic standpoint that he might have violated it had he lived longer. My certainty rests upon the knowledge in depth I have of the other and of my own experience of love and integrity. This kind of knowledge is possible only to the extent that I can drop my own ego and see the other man in *his* suchness, recognize the structure of forces in him, see him in his individuality and at the same time in his universal humanity. Then I know what the other can do, what he cannot do, and what he will not do. Of course, I do not mean by this that I could predict all his future behavior, but only the general lines of behavior that are rooted in basic character traits, such as integrity, responsibility, etc. (See the chapter on "Faith as a Character Trait" in *Man for Himself.*)

This faith is based on facts; hence it is rational. But the facts are not recognizable or "provable" by the method of conventional, positivistic psychology; I, the alive person, am the only instrument that can "register" them.

Loving

Loving also has two meanings, depending upon whether it is spoken of in the mode of having or in the mode of being.

Can one *have* love? If we could, love would need to be a thing, a substance that one can have, own, possess. The truth is, there is no such thing as "love." "Love" is an abstraction, perhaps a goddess or an alien being, although nobody has ever seen this goddess. In reality, there exists only the *act of loving.* To love is a productive activity. It implies caring for, knowing, responding, affirming, enjoying: the person, the tree, the painting, the idea. It means bringing to life, increasing his/her/its aliveness. It is a process, self-renewing and self-increasing.

When love is experienced in the mode of having it implies confining, imprisoning, or controlling the object one "loves." It is strangling, deadening, suffocating, killing, not life-giving. What people *call* love is mostly a misuse of the word, in order to hide the reality of their not loving. How many parents love their children is still an entirely open question. Lloyd de Mause has brought out that for the past two millennia of Western history there have been reports of cruelty against children, ranging from physical to psychic torture, carelessness, sheer possessiveness, and sadism so shocking that one must believe that loving parents are the exception rather than the rule.

The same may be said of marriages. Whether their marriage is based on love or, like traditional marriages of the past, on social convenience and custom, the couple who truly love each other seem to be the exception. What is social convenience, custom, mutual economic interest, shared interest in children, mutual dependency, or mutual hate or fear is consciously experienced as "love"—up to the moment when one or both partners recognize that they do not love each other, and that they never did. Today one can note some progress in this respect: people have become more realistic and sober, and many no longer feel that being sexually attracted means to love, or that a friendly, though distant, team relationship is a manifestation of loving. This new outlook has made for greater honesty—as well as more frequent change of partners. It has not necessarily led to a greater frequency of loving, and the new partners may love as little as did the old.

The change from "falling in love" to the illusion of "having" love can often be observed in concrete detail in the history of couples who have "fallen in love." (In *The Art of Loving* I pointed out that the word "falling" in the phrase "falling in love" is a contradiction in itself. Since loving is a productive activity, one can only *stand* in love or *walk* in love; one cannot "fall" in love, for falling denotes passivity.)

During courtship neither person is yet sure of the other, but each tries to win the other. Both are alive, attractive, interesting, even beautiful—inasmuch as aliveness always makes a face beautiful. Neither yet *has* the other; hence each one's energy is directed to *being,* i.e., to giving to and stimulating the other. With the act of marriage the situation frequently changes fundamentally. The marriage contract gives each partner the exclusive possession of the other's body, feelings, and care. Nobody has to be won over any more, because love has become something one *has,* a property. The two cease to make the effort to be lovable and to produce love, hence they become boring, and hence their beauty disappears. They are disappointed and puzzled. Are they not the same persons any more? Did they make a mistake in the first place? Each usually seeks the cause of the change in the other and feels defrauded. What they do not see is that they no longer are the same people they were when they were in love with each other; that the error that one can *have* love has led them to cease loving. Now, instead of loving each other, they settle for owning together what they have: money, social standing, a home, children. Thus, in some cases, the marriage initiated on the basis of love becomes transformed into a friendly ownership, a corporation in which the two egotisms are pooled into one: that of the "family."

When a couple cannot get over the yearning for the renewal of the previous feeling of loving, one or the other of the pair may have the illusion that a new partner (or partners) will satisfy their longing. They feel that all they want to have is love. But love to them is not an expression of their being; it is a goddess to whom they want to submit. They necessarily fail with their love because "love is a child of liberty" (as an old French songs says), and the worshiper of the goddess of love eventually becomes so passive as to be boring and loses whatever is left of his or her former attractiveness.

This description is not intended to imply that marriage

cannot be the best solution for two people who love each other. The difficulty does not lie in marriage, but in the possessive, existential structure of both partners and, in the last analysis, of their society. The advocates of such modern-day forms of living together as group marriage, changing partners, group sex, etc., try, as far as I can see, only to avoid the problem of their difficulties in loving by curing boredom with ever new stimuli and by wanting *to have* more "lovers," rather than to be able to love even one. (See the discussion of the distinction between "activating" and "passivating" stimuli in Chapter 10 of *The Anatomy of Human Destructiveness*.)

III

HAVING AND BEING IN THE OLD AND NEW TESTAMENTS AND IN THE WRITINGS OF MASTER ECKHART

The Old Testament

One of the main themes of the Old Testament is: leave what you have; free yourself from all fetters; *be!*

The history of Hebrew tribes begins with the command to the first Hebrew hero, *Abraham,* to give up his country and his clan: "Go from your country and your kindred and your father's house to the land that I will show you" (Genesis 12:1). Abraham is to leave what he has—land and family—and go to the unknown. Yet his descendants settle on a new soil, and new clannishness develops. This process leads to more severe bondage. Precisely because they become rich and powerful in Egypt, they become slaves; they lose the vision of the one God, the God of their nomadic ancestors, and they worship idols, the gods of the rich turned later into their masters.

The second hero is *Moses.* He is charged by God to liberate his people, to lead them out of the country that has become their home (even though eventually a home for slaves), and to go into the desert "to celebrate." Reluctantly and with great misgiving, the Hebrews follow their leader Moses—into the desert.

The desert is the key symbol in this liberation. The desert is no home: it has no cities; it has no riches; it is the place of nomads who own what they need, and what they need are the necessities of life, not possessions. Historically, nomadic traditions are interwoven in the report of the Exodus, and it may very well be that these nomadic traditions have determined the tendency against all nonfunctional property and the choice of life in the desert as preparation for the life of freedom. But these historical factors only strengthen the meaning of the desert as a symbol of the unfettered, nonpropertied life. Some of the main symbols of the Jewish festivals have their origin in the connection with the desert. The *unleavened bread* is the bread of those who are in a hurry to leave; it is the bread of the wanderers. The *suka* ("tabernacle") is the home of the wanderer: the equivalent of the tent, easily built and easily taken down. As defined in the Talmud it is "the transitory abode," to be lived in, instead of the "fixed abode" one owns.

The Hebrews yearn for the fleshpots of Egypt; for the fixed home, for the poor yet guaranteed food; for the visible idols. They fear the uncertainty of the propertyless desert life. They say: "Would that we had died by the hand of the Lord in the land of Egypt, when we sat by the fleshpots and ate bread to the full; for you have brought us out into this wilderness to kill this whole assembly with hunger" (Exodus: 16:3). God, as in the whole story of liberation, responds to the moral frailty of the people. He promises to feed them: in the morning with "bread," in the evening with quail. He adds two important injunctions: each should gather according to their needs: "And the people of Israel did so; they gathered, some more, some less. But when they measured it with an omer, he that gathered much had nothing over, and he that gathered little had no lack; each gathered according to what he could eat" (Exodus 16:17–18).

For the first time, a principle is formulated here that became famous through Marx: to each according to their needs. The right to be fed was established without qualification. God is here the nourishing mother who feeds her children, who do not have to achieve anything in order to

establish their right to be fed. The second injunction is
one against hoarding, greed, and possessiveness. The people of Israel were enjoined not to save anything till the
next morning. "But they did not listen to Moses; some left
part of it till the morning, and it bred worms and became
foul; and Moses was angry with them. Morning by morning they gathered it, each as much as he could eat; but
when the sun grew hot, it melted" (Exodus 16:20–21).

In connection with the collection of food the concept of
the observation of the *Shabbat* ("Sabbath") is intro-
duced. Moses tells the Hebrews to collect twice the usual
amount of food on Friday: "Six days you shall gather it;
but on the seventh day, which is a Sabbath, there will be
none" (Exodus 16:26).

The Shabbat is the most important of the biblical
concepts, and of later Judaism. It is the only strictly
religious command in the Ten Commandments: its fulfillment is insisted upon by the otherwise antiritualistic
prophets; it was a most strictly observed commandment
throughout 2000 years of Diaspora life, wherein its observation often was hard and difficult. It can hardly be
doubted that the Shabbat was the fountain of life for the
Jews, who, scattered, powerless, and often despised and
persecuted, renewed their pride and dignity when like
kings they celebrated the Shabbat. Is the Shabbat nothing
but a day of rest in the mundane sense of freeing people,
at least on one day, from the burden of work? To be sure
it is that, and this function gives it the dignity of one of
the great innovations in human evolution. Yet if this were
all that it was, the Shabbat would hardly have played the
central role I have just described.

In order to understand this role we must penetrate to
the core of the Shabbat institution. It is not rest *per se,* in
the sense of not making an effort, physically or mentally.
It is rest in the sense of the re-establishment of complete
harmony between human beings and between them and
nature. Nothing must be destroyed and nothing be built:
the Shabbat is a day of truce in the human battle with the
world. Even tearing up a blade of grass is looked upon as
a breach of this harmony, as is lighting a match. Neither
must social change occur. It is for this reason that carry-

ing anything on the street is forbidden (even if it weighs
as little as a handkerchief), while carrying a heavy load
in one's garden is permitted. The point is that not the
effort of carrying a load is forbidden, but the transfer of
any object from one privately owned piece of land to
another, because such transfer constituted, originally, a
transfer of property. On the Shabbat one lives as if one
has nothing, pursuing no aim except *being,* that is, expressing one's essential powers: praying, studying, eating,
drinking, singing, making love.

The Shabbat is a day of joy because on that day one is
fully oneself. This is the reason the Talmud calls a Shabbat the anticipation of the Messianic Time, and the Messianic Time the unending Shabbat: the day on which
property and money as well as mourning and sadness are
tabu; a day on which time is defeated and pure being
rules. The historical predecessor, the Babylonian Shapatu,
was a day of sadness and fear. The modern Sunday is a
day of fun, consumption, and running away from oneself.
One might ask if it is not time to re-establish the Shabbat
as a universal day of harmony and peace, as the human
day that anticipates the human future.

The vision of the Messianic Time is the other specifically Jewish contribution to world culture, and one essentially identical with that of the Shabbat. This vision, like
the Shabbat, was the life-sustaining hope of the Jews,
never given up in spite of the severe disappointments that
came with the false messiahs, from Bar Kochba in the
second century to our days. Like the Shabbat it was a
vision of a historical period in which possession will have
become meaningless, fear and war will have ended, and
the expression of our essential powers will have become
the aim of living.*

The history of the Exodus moves to a tragic end. The
Hebrews cannot bear to live without *having.* Although
they can live without a fixed abode, and without food

---

*I have analyzed the concept of Messianic Time in *You Shall Be
as Gods.* The Shabbat, too, is discussed in that earlier book, as well
as in the chapter on "The Sabbath Ritual" in *The Forgotten
Language.*

except that sent by God every day, they cannot live without a visible, present "leader."

Thus when Moses disappears on the mountain, the desperate Hebrews get Aaron to make them a visible manifestation of something they can worship: the Golden Calf. Here, one may say, they pay for God's error in having permitted them to take gold and jewelry out of Egypt. With the gold, they carried within themselves the craving for wealth; and when the hour of despair came, the possessive structure of their existence reasserted itself. Aaron makes them a calf from the gold, and the people say: "These are your Gods, O Israel, who brought you up out of the land of Egypt" (Exodus 32:4).

A whole generation had died and even Moses was not permitted to enter the new land. But the new generation was as little capable of being unfettered and of living on a land without being bound to it as were their fathers. They conquer new land, exterminate their enemies, settle on their soil, and worship their idols. They transform their democratic tribal life into that of Oriental despotism— small, indeed, but not less eager to imitate the great powers of the day. The revolution had failed; its only achievement was, if it was one, that the Hebrews were now masters and not slaves. They might not even be remembered today, except as a learned footnote in a history of the Near East, had the new message not found expression through revolutionary thinkers and visionaries who were not tainted, as was Moses, by the burden of leadership and specifically by the need to use dictatorial power methods (for instance the wholesale destruction of the rebels under Korach).

These revolutionary thinkers, the Hebrew prophets, renewed the vision of human freedom—of being unfettered of things—and the protest against submitting to idols—the work of the people's own hands. They were uncompromising and predicted that the people would have to be expelled from the land again if they became incestuously fixated to it and incapable of living in it as free people—that is, not able to love it without losing themselves in it. To the prophets the expulsion from the land was a tragedy, but the only way to final liberation; the new desert was to last not for one but for many generations. Even while predicting the new desert, the prophets were sustaining the faith of the Jews, and eventually of the whole human race, by the Messianic vision that promised peace and abundance without requiring the expulsion or extermination of a land's former inhabitants.

The real successors to the Hebrew prophets were the great scholars, the rabbis, and none more clearly so than the founder of the Diaspora: Rabbi Jochanan ben Sakai. When the leaders of the war against the Romans (A.D. 70) had decided that it was better for all to die than to be defeated and lose their state, Rabbi Sakai committed "treason." He secretly left Jerusalem, surrendered to the Roman general, and asked permission to found a Jewish university. This was the beginning of a rich Jewish tradition and, at the same time, of the loss of everything the Jews had *had*: their state, their temple, their priestly and military bureaucracy, their sacrificial animals, and their rituals. All were lost and they were left (as a group) with nothing except the ideal of being: knowing, learning, thinking, and hoping for the Messiah.

The New Testament

The New Testament continues the Old Testament's protest against the having structure of existence. Its protest is even more radical than the earlier Jewish protest had been. The Old Testament was not the product of a poor and downtrodden class, but sprang from nomadic sheepowners and independent peasants. A millennium later, the Pharisees, the learned men whose literary product was the Talmud, represented the middle class, ranging from some very poor to some very well-to-do members. Both groups were imbued with the spirit of social justice, the protection of the poor, and the assistance to all who were powerless, such as widows and national minorities (*gerim*). But on the whole, they did not condemn wealth as evil or as incompatible with the principle of being. (See Louis Finkelstein's book on *The Pharisees*.)

Earliest Christians, on the contrary, were mainly a group of the poor and socially despised, of the downtrodden and outcasts, who—like some of the Old Testament prophets—castigated the rich and powerful, denouncing without compromise wealth and secular and priestly power, as unmitigated evils (see *The Dogma of Christ*). Indeed, as Max Weber said, the Sermon on the Mount was the speech of a great slave rebellion. The mood of the early Christians was one of full human solidarity, sometimes expressed in the idea of a spontaneous communal sharing of all material goods. (A. F. Utz discusses the early Christian communal ownership and earlier Greek examples of whom Luke probably knew.)

This revolutionary spirit of early Christianity appears with special clarity in the oldest parts of the gospels as they were known to the Christian communities that still had not separated from Judaism. (Those oldest parts of the gospels can be reconstructed from the common source of Matthew and Luke and are called "Q" [Q from German *Quelle*, "source"] by specialists in the history of the New Testament. The fundamental work in this field is by Siegried Schulz, who differentiates between an older and a younger tradition of "Q.")*

In these sayings we find as the central postulate that people must free themselves from all greed and cravings for possession and must totally liberate themselves from the structure of having, and conversely, that all positive ethical norms are rooted in an ethics of being, sharing, and solidarity. This basic ethical position is applied both to one's relations to others and to one's relations to things. The radical renunciation of one's own rights (Matthew 5:39–42; Luke 6:29 f.) as well as the command to love one's enemy (Matthew 5:44–48; Luke 6:27 f., 32–36) stress, even more radically than the Old Testament's "love thy neighbor," full concern for other human beings and complete surrender of all selfishness. The norm not even to judge others (Matthew 7:1–5; Luke 6:37 f., 41 f.) is a further extension of the principle

*I am indebted to Rainer Funk for his thorough information about this field and for his fruitful suggestions.

of forgetting one's ego and being totally devoted to the understanding and the well-being of the other.

Also with regard to things, total renunciation of the having structure is demanded. The oldest community insisted on the radical renunciation of property; it warns against collecting riches: "Do not lay up for yourselves treasures on earth, where moth and rust consume and where thieves break in and steal, but lay up for yourselves treasures in heaven, where neither moth nor rust consumes and where thieves do not break in and steal. For where your treasure is, there will your heart be also" (Matthew 6:19–21; Luke 12:33 f.). It is in the same spirit that Jesus says: "Blessed are you poor for yours is the kingdom of God" (Luke 6:20; Matthew 5:3). Indeed, early Christianity was a community of the poor and the suffering, filled with the apocalyptic conviction that the time had come for the final disappearance of the existing order, according to God's plan of salvation.

The apocalyptic concept of the "Last Judgment" was one version of the Messianic idea, current in Jewish circles of the time. Final salvation and judgment would be preceded by a period of chaos and destruction, a period so terrible that we find Talmudic rabbis asking God to spare them living in the pre-Messianic Time. What was new in Christianity was that Jesus and his followers believed that the Time was *now* (or in the near future), and that it had already begun with Jesus' appearance.

Indeed, one cannot help associating the situation of the early Christians with what goes on in the world today. Not a few people, scientists rather than religionists (with the exception of the Jehovah's Witnesses), believe that we might be approaching the final catastrophe of the world. This is a rational and scientifically tenable vision. The situation of the early Christians was quite different. They lived in a small part of the Roman Empire at the height of its power and glory. There were no alarming signs of catastrophe. Yet this small group of poor Palestinian Jews carried the conviction that this powerful world would soon collapse. Realistically, to be sure, they were mistaken; as a result of the failure of Jesus' reappearance, Jesus' death and resurrection are interpreted in the gospels as constituting the beginning of the new eon, and after Constantine an attempt was made to shift the mediating role of Jesus to the papal church. Finally, for all practical purposes the church became the substitute—in fact, though not in theory—for the new eon.

One must take early Christianity more seriously than most people do, in order to be impressed by the almost unbelievable radicalism of this small group of people, who spoke the verdict over the existing world on *nothing but* their moral conviction. The majority of the Jews, on the other hand, not belonging exclusively to the poorest and most downtrodden part of the population, chose another way. They refused to believe that a new era had begun and continued to wait for the Messiah, who would come when humankind (and not only the Jews) had reached the point where the realm of justice, peace, and love could be established in a historical rather than in an eschatological sense.

The younger "Q" source has its origin in a further stage of development of early Christianity. Here, too, we find the same principle, and the story of Jesus' temptation by Satan expresses it in a very succinct form. In this story, the lust for having things and the craving for power and other manifestations of the having structure are condemned. To the first temptation—to transform stones into bread, symbolically expressing the craving for material things—Jesus answers: "Man shall not live by bread alone, but by every word that proceeds from the mouth of God" (Matthew 4:4; Luke 4:4). Satan tempts Jesus then with the promise of giving him complete power over nature (changing the law of gravity), and finally, with unrestricted power, dominion over all kingdoms of the earth, and Jesus declines (Matthew 4:5–10; Luke 4:5–12). (Rainer Funk has called my attention to the fact that the temptation takes place in the desert, thus taking up the topic of the Exodus again.)

Jesus and Satan appear here as representatives of two opposite principles. Satan is the representative of material consumption and of power over nature and Man. Jesus is the representative of being, and of the idea that not-having is the premise for being. The world has followed Satan's principles, since the time of the gospels. Yet even the victory of these principles could not destroy the longing for the realization of full being, expressed by Jesus as well as by many other great Masters who lived before him and after him.

The ethical rigorism of rejection of the having orientation for the sake of the being orientation is to be found also in the Jewish communal orders, such as the Essenes and the order in which the Dead Sea scrolls originated. Throughout the history of Christianity it continues in the religious orders based on the vow of poverty and property-lessness.

Another manifestation of the radical concepts of early Christianity is to be found—in various degrees—in the writings of the church fathers, who in this respect are also influenced by Greek philosophical thought on the subject of private property versus common property. Space does not permit me to discuss these teachings in any detail, and even less the theological and sociological literature on the subject.* Although there are some differences in the degree of radicalism and a certain trend to a less radical view the more the church became a powerful institution, it is undeniable that the early church thinkers shared a sharp condemnation of luxury and avarice and a contempt for wealth.

Justin writes, in the middle of the second century: "We who once loved riches [mobile goods] and possession [land] above everything else, now make that which we already have into common property and share it with the needy." In a "Letter of Diognetus" (also second century), there is a very interesting passage that reminds us of Old Testament thought about homelessness: "Any alien country is their [the Christians'] fatherland and every fatherland is alien to them." Tertullian (third century) considered all trade to be the result of cupidity, and

*See the contributions of A. F. Utz, O. Schilling, H. Schumacher, and others.

he denies its necessity among people who are free from greed. He declares that trade always carries with it the danger of idolatry. Avarice he calls the root of all evil.*

For Basilius, as for the other church fathers, the purpose of all material goods is to serve people; characteristic of him is this question: "The one who takes away a garment from another is called a thief; but the one who does not clothe the poor, although he could—does he deserve another name?" (quoted by Utz). Basilius stressed the original community of goods and was understood by some authors to have represented communist tendencies. I conclude this brief sketch with Chrysostomus' warning (fourth century) that superfluous goods must not be produced or consumed. He says: "Do not say I use what is mine: you use what is alien to you; the indulgent, selfish use makes what is yours something alien; that is why I call it alien good, because you use it with a hardened heart and claim that it is right, that you alone live from what is yours."

I could go on for many pages quoting the views of the church fathers that private property and the egotistical use of any possession is immoral. Yet even the foregoing few statements indicate the continuity of the rejection of the having orientation as we find it from Old Testament times, throughout early Christianity, and into the later centuries. Even Aquinas, battling against the openly communist sects, concludes that the institution of private property is justified only inasmuch as it best serves the purposes of satisfying the welfare of all.

Classic Buddhism emphasizes even more strongly than the Old and New Testaments the central importance of giving up craving for possessions of any kind, including one's own ego, the concept of a lasting substance, and even the craving for one's perfection.†

---

*The above passages are taken from Otto Schilling; see also his quotations from K. Farner and T. Sommerlad.

†For a penetrating understanding of Buddhism, see the writings of Nyanaponika Mahatera, particularly *The Heart of Buddhist Meditation* and *Pathways of Buddhist Thought: Essays from the Wheel.*

Master Eckhart (1260–c. 1327)

Eckhart has described and analyzed the difference between the having and being modes of existence with a penetration and clarity not surpassed by any teacher. A major figure of the Dominican Order in Germany, Eckhart was a scholarly theologian and the greatest representative and deepest and most radical thinker of German mysticism. His greatest influence radiated from his German sermons, which affected not only his contemporaries and disciples but also German mystics after him and, today, those seeking authentic guidance to a nontheistic, rational, yet religious, philosophy of life.

My sources for the Eckhart quotations that follow are Joseph L. Quint's great Eckhart work *Meister Eckhart, Die Deutschen Werke* (referred to here as "Quint D.W."), his *Meister Eckhart, Deutsche Predigten und Traktate* (referred to as "Quint D.P.T."), and the English translation by Raymond B. Blakney, *Meister Eckhart* (referred to here as "Blakney"). It should be noted that while Quint's editions contain only the passages he considers have been proven authentic so far, the Blakney text (translated from the German, Pfeiffer, edition) includes writings whose authenticity Quint has not yet acknowledged. Quint himself has pointed out, however, that his recognition of authenticity is provisional, that very likely many of the other works that have been attributed to Master Eckhart will also be proven authentic. The italicized numbers that appear with the source notes refer to the Eckhart sermons as they are identified in the three sources.

Eckhart's Concept of Having

The classic source for Eckhart's views on the mode of having is his sermon on poverty, based on the text of Matthew 5:13: "Blessed are the poor in spirit, for theirs is the kingdom of heaven." In this sermon Eckhart discusses the question: What is spiritual poverty? He begins by saying that he does not speak of *external* poverty, a poverty of things, although that kind of poverty is good and commendable. He wants to speak of *inner* poverty, the poverty referred to in the gospel verse, which he defines by saying: "He is a poor man who *wants* nothing, *knows* nothing and *has* nothing" (Blakney, *28;* Quint D.W., *52;* Quint D.P.T., *32*).

Who is the person who *wants* nothing? A man or woman who has chosen an ascetic life would be our common response. But this is not Eckhart's meaning, and he scolds those who understand not wanting anything as an exercise of repentance and an external religious practice. He sees the subscribers to that concept as people who hold onto their selfish egos. "These people have the name of being saintly on the basis of the external appearances, but inside they are asses, because they don't grasp the true meaning of divine truth" (my translation of Quint's text).

For Eckhart is concerned with the kind of "wanting" that is also fundamental in Buddhist thought; that is, greed, craving for things and for one's own ego. The Buddha considers this wanting (attachment, craving) to be the cause of human suffering, not of enjoyment. When Eckhart goes on to speak of having no will, he does not mean that one should be weak. The will he speaks of is identical with craving, a will that one is *driven* by—that is, in a true sense, *not* will. Eckhart goes as far as to postulate that one should not even want to do God's will—since this, too, is a form of craving. *The person who wants nothing is the person who is not greedy for anything*: this is the essence of Eckhart's concept of nonattachment.

Who is the person who *knows* nothing? Does Eckhart establish that it is one who is an ignorant dumb being, an uneducated, uncultured creature? How could he, when his main effort was to educate the uneducated and when he himself was a man of great erudition and knowledge that he never attempts to hide or minimize?

Eckhart's concept of *not knowing anything* is concerned with the difference between *having* knowledge and the *act* of *knowing,* i.e., penetrating to the roots and, hence, to the causes of a thing. Eckhart distinguishes very clearly between a particular thought and the *process* of thinking. Stressing that it is better to know God than to love God, he writes: "Love has to do with desire and purpose, whereas knowledge is no particular thought, but rather it peels off all [coverings] and is disinterested and runs naked to God, until it touches him and grasps him" (Blakney, Fragment 27; not authenticated by Quint).

But on another level (and Eckhart speaks throughout on several levels) Eckhart goes much further. He writes:

> Again, he is poor who knows nothing. We have some-times said that man ought to live as if he did not live, neither for self, nor for the truth, nor for God. But to that point, we shall say something else and go further. The man who is to achieve this poverty shall live as a man who does not even know that he lives, neither for himself, nor for the truth, nor for god. More; he shall be quit and empty of all knowledge, so that no knowledge of god exists in him; for when a man's existence is of God's external species, there is no other life in him: his life is himself. Therefore we say that a man ought to be empty of his own knowledge, as he was when he did not exist, and let God achieve what he will and man be unfettered (Blakney, *28;* Quint D.W., *52;* Quint D.P.T., *32;* a small portion is my translation of Quint's German text).*

To understand Eckhart's position, it is necessary to grasp the true meaning of these words. When he says that "a man ought to be empty of his own knowledge," he does not mean that one should forget *what* one knows, but rather one should forget *that* one knows. This is to say that we should not look at our knowledge as a possession, in which we find security and which gives us a sense of identity; we should not be "filled" with our knowledge, or hang onto it, or crave it. Knowledge should

---

*Blakney uses a capital "G" for God when Eckhart refers to the Godhead and a lower-case "g" when Eckhart refers to the biblical god of creation.

not assume the quality of a dogma, which enslaves us. All this belongs to the mode of having. In the mode of being, knowledge is nothing but the penetrating activity of thought—without ever becoming an invitation to stand still in order to find certainty. Eckhart continues:

> What does it mean that a man should *have* nothing? Now pay earnest attention to this: I have often said, and great authorities agree, that to be a proper abode for God and fit for God to act in, a man should also be free from all [his own] things and [his own] actions, both inwardly and outwardly. Now we shall say something else. If it is the case that a man is emptied of things, creatures, himself and god, and if still God could find a place in him to act, then we say: As long as that [place] exists, this man is not poor with the most intimate poverty. For God does not intend that man shall have a place reserved for God to work in, since true poverty of spirit requires that man shall be emptied of God and all his works, so that if God wants to act in the soul, he himself must be the place in which he acts— and that he would like to do. . . . Thus we say that a man should be so poor that he is not and has not a place for God to act in. To reserve a place would be to maintain distinctions. *Therefore I pray God that he may quit me of god"* (Blakney, pp. 230–231).

Eckhart could not have expressed his concept of not having more radically. First of all, we should be free from our own things and our own actions. This does not mean that we should neither possess anything nor do anything; it means we should not be bound, tied, chained to what we own and what we have, not even to God.

Eckhart approaches the problems of having on another level when he discusses the relation between possession and freedom. Human freedom is restricted to the extent to which we are bound to possession, works, and lastly, to our own egos. By being bound to our egos (Quint translates the original middle-German *Eigenschaft* as *Ich-bindung* or *Ichsucht,* "egoboundness" or "egomania"), we stand in our own way and are blocked from bearing fruit, from realizing ourselves fully (Quint D.P.T., Introduction, p. 29). D. Mieth, in my opinion, is entirely right when he maintains that freedom as a condition of true productivity is nothing but giving up one's ego, as love in the Paulinian sense is free from all egoboundness. Freedom in the sense of being unfettered, free from the craving for holding onto things and one's ego, is the condition for love and for productive being. Our human aim, according to Eckhart, is to get rid of the fetters of egoboundness, egocentricity, that is to say the *having mode* of existence, in order to arrive at full being. I have not found any author whose thoughts about the nature of the having orientation in Eckhart are as similar to my own thinking as those expressed by Mieth (1971). He speaks of the *Besitzstruktur des Menschen* ("the property structure of the people") in the same way, as far as I can see, that I speak of the "having mode," or the "having structure of existence." He refers to the Marxian concept of "expropriation," when he speaks of the breakthrough of one's own inner property structure, adding that it is the most radical form of expropriation.

In the having mode of existence what matters is not the various *objects* of having, but our whole attitude. Everything and anything can become an object of craving: things we use in daily life, property, rituals, good deeds, knowledge, and thoughts. While they are not in themselves "bad," they become bad; that is, when we hold onto them, when they become chains that interfere with our freedom, they block our self-realization.

Eckhart's Concept of Being

Eckhart uses being in two different, though related, meanings. In a narrower, psychological sense, being denotes the *real* and often unconscious motivations that impel human beings, in contrast to deeds and opinions as such and separated from the acting and thinking person. Quint justly calls Eckhart an extraordinary analyst of the soul (*genialer Seelenanalytiker*): "Eckhart never tires of uncovering the most secret ties of human behavior, the most hidden stirring of selfishness, of intentions and opinions, of denouncing the passionate longing for gratitude and rewards" (Quint D.P.T., Introduction, p. 29; my translation). This insight into the hidden motives makes Eckhart most appealing to the post-Freudian reader, who has overcome the naïveté of pre-Freudian and still current behavioristic views, which claim that behavior and opinion are two final data that can be as little broken down as the atom was supposed to be at the beginning of this century. Eckhart expressed this view in numerous statements, of which the following is characteristic: "People should not consider so much what they are to *do* as what they *are*. . . . Thus take care that your emphasis is laid on *being* good and not on the number of kind of things to be done. Emphasize rather the fundamentals on which your work rests." Our being is the reality, the spirit that moves us, the character that impels our behavior; in contrast, the deeds or opinions that are separated from our dynamic core have no reality.

The second meaning is wider and more fundamental: being is life, activity, birth, renewal, outpouring, flowing out, productivity. In this sense, being is the opposite of having, of egoboundness and egotism. Being, to Eckhart, means to be active in the classic sense of the productive expression of one's human powers, not in the modern sense of being busy. Activity to him means "to go out of oneself" (Quint D.P.T., 6; my translation), which he expresses in many word pictures: he calls being a process of "boiling," of "giving birth," something that "flows and flows in itself and beyond itself" (E. Benz et al., quoted in Quint D.P.T., p. 35; my translation). Sometimes he uses the symbol of running in order to indicate the active character: "Run into peace! The man who is in the state of running, of continuous running into peace is a heavenly man. He continually runs and moves and seeks peace in running" (Quint D.P.T., 8; my translation). Another definition of activity is: The active, alive man is like a "vessel that grows as it is filled and will never be full" (Blakney, p. 233; not authenticated by Quint).

Breaking through the mode of having is the condition for all genuine activity. In Eckhart's ethical system the supreme virtue is the state of productive inner acvitity, for which the premise is the overcoming of all forms of egoboundness and craving.

PART TWO

ANALYZING THE FUNDAMENTAL DIFFERENCES BETWEEN THE TWO MODES OF EXISTENCE

IV

WHAT IS THE HAVING MODE?

The Acquisitive Society—Basis for the Having Mode

Our judgments are extremely biased because we live in a society that rests on private property, profit, and power as the pillars of its existence. To acquire, to own, and to make a profit are the sacred and unalienable rights of the individual in the industrial society.* What the sources of property are does not matter; nor does possession impose any obligations on the property owners. The principle is: "Where and how my property was acquired or what I do with it is nobody's business but my own; as long as I do not violate the law, my right is unrestricted and absolute."

This kind of property may be called *private* property (from Latin *privare*, "to deprive of"), because the person or persons who own it are its sole masters, with full power to deprive others of its use or enjoyment. While private ownership is supposed to be a natural and universal category, it is in fact an exception rather than the rule if we consider the whole of human history (including prehistory), and particularly the cultures outside Europe in

*R. H. Tawney's 1920 work, *The Acquisitive Society,* is still unsurpassed in its understanding of modern capitalism and options for social and human change. The contributions by Max Weber, Brentano, Schapiro, Pascal, Sombart, and Kraus contain fundamental insights for understanding industrial society's influence on human beings.

which economy was not life's main concern. Aside from private property, there are: *self-created* property, which is exclusively the result of one's own work; *restricted property,* which is *restricted* by the obligation to help one's fellow beings; *functional,* or *personal,* property, which consists either of tools for work or of objects for enjoyment; *common* property, which a group shares in the spirit of a common bond, such as the Israeli kibbutzim.

The norms by which society functions also mold the character of its members ("social character"). In an industrial society these are: the wish to acquire property, to keep it, and to increase it, i.e., to make a profit, and those who own property are admired and envied as superior beings. But the vast majority of people own no property in a real sense of capital and capital goods, and the puzzling question arises: How can such people fulfill or even cope with their passion for acquiring and keeping property, or how can they feel like owners of property when they haven't any property to speak of?

Of course, the obvious answer is that even people who are property poor own *something*—and they cherish their little possessions as much as the owners of capital cherish their property. And like the big property owners, the poor are obsessed by the wish to preserve what they do have and to increase it, even though by an infinitesimal amount (for instance by saving a penny here, two cents there).

Furthermore the greatest enjoyment perhaps is not so much in owning material things but in owning living beings. In a patriarchal society even the most miserable of men in the poorest of classes can be an owner of property—in his relationship to his wife, his children, his animals, over whom he can feel he is absolute master. At least for the man in a patriarchal society, having many children is the only way to own persons without needing to work to attain ownership, and with little capital investment. Considering that the whole burden of childbearing is the woman's, it can hardly be denied that the production of children in a patriarchal society is a matter of crude exploitation of women. In turn, however, the mothers have their own form of ownership, that of the children when they are small. The circle is endless and vicious: the husband exploits the wife, she exploits the small children, and the adolescent males soon join the elder men in exploiting the women, and so on.

The male hegemony in a patriarchal order has lasted roughly six or seven millennia and still prevails in the poorest countries and among the poorest classes of society. It is, however, slowly diminishing in the more affluent societies—emancipation of women, children, and adolescents seems to take place when and to the degree that a society's standard of living rises. With the slow collapse of the old-fashioned, patriarchal type of ownership of persons, in what will the average citizens of the fully developed industrial societies now find fulfillment of their passion for acquiring, keeping, and increasing property? The answer lies in extending the area of ownership to include friends, lovers, health, travel, art objects, God, one's own ego. A brilliant picture of the bourgeois obsession with property is given by Max Stirner. Persons are transformed into things; their relations to each other assume the character of ownership. "Individualism," which in its positive sense means liberation from social chains, means, in the negatives sense, "self-ownership," the right—and the duty —to invest one's energy in the success of one's own person.

Our ego is the most important object of our property feeling, for it comprises many things: our body, our name, our social status, our possessions (including our knowledge), the image we have of ourselves and the image we want others to have of us. Our ego is a mixture of real qualities, such as knowledge and skills, and of certain fictitious qualities that we build around a core of reality. But the essential point is not so much what the ego's content is, but that the ego is felt as a thing we each possess, and that this "thing" is the basis of our sense of identity.

This discussion of property must take into account that an important form of property attachment that flourished in the nineteenth century has been diminishing in the decades since the end of the First World War and is little evident today. In the older period, everything one owned was cherished, taken care of, and used to the very limits of its utility. Buying was "keep-it" buying, and a motto for the nineteenth century might well have been: "Old is beautiful!" Today, consumption is emphasized, not preservation, and buying has become "throw-away" buying. Whether the object one buys is a car, a dress, a gadget, after using it for some time, one gets tired of it and is eager to dispose of the "old" and buy the latest model. Acquisition → transitory having and using → throwing away (or if possible, profitable exchange for a better model) → new acquisition, constitutes the vicious circle of consumer-buying and today's motto could indeed be: "New is beautiful!"

Perhaps the most striking example of today's consumer-buying phenomenon is the private automobile. Our age deserves to be dubbed "the age of the automobile," for our whole economy has been built around automobile production, and our whole life is greatly determined by the rise and fall of the consumer market for cars.

To those who have one, their car seems like a vital necessity; to those who do not yet own one, especially people in the so-called socialist states, a car is a symbol of happiness. Apparently, however, affection for one's car is not deep and abiding, but a love affair of somewhat short duration, for owners change their cars frequently; after two years, even after just one, an auto owner tires of the "old car" and starts shopping around for a "good deal" on a new vehicle. From shopping around to purchase, the whole transaction seems to be a game in which even trickery is sometimes a prime element, and the "good deal" is enjoyed as much as, if not more than, the ultimate prize: that brand-new model in the driveway.

Several factors must be taken into acount in order to solve the puzzle of the seemingly flagrant contradiction between the owners' property relationship to their automobiles and their so-short-lived interest in them. First, there is the element of depersonalization in the owner's relationship to the car; the car is not a concrete object that its owner is fond of, but a status symbol, an extension of power—an ego builder; having acquired a car, the owner has actually acquired a new piece of ego. A second factor is that buying a new car every two years instead of, say, every six increases the buyer's thrill of acquisition; the act of making the new car one's own is a kind of defloration—it enhances one's sense of control, and the more often it happens, the more thrilled one is. The third factor is that frequent car buying means frequent opportunities to "make a deal"—to make a profit by the exchange—a satisfaction deeply rooted in men and women today. The fourth factor is one of great importance: the need to experience *new* stimuli, because the old stimuli are flat and exhausted after but a short while. In an earlier discussion of stimuli (*The Anatomy of Human Destructiveness*), I differentiated between "activating" and "passivating" stimuli and suggested the following formulation: "The more 'passivating' a stimulus is, the more frequently it must be changed in intensity and/or in kind; the more 'activating' it is, the longer it retains its stimulating quality and the less necessary is change in intensity and content." The fifth and most important factor lies in the change in social character that has occurred during the last hundred years, i.e., from the "hoarding" to the "marketing" character. While the change does not do away with the having orientation, it does modify it considerably. (This development from the hoarding to the marketing character is discussed in Chapter VII.)

The proprietary feeling also shows up in other relationships, for example toward doctors, dentists, lawyers, bosses, workers. People express it in speaking of "*my* doctor," "*my* dentist," "*my* workers," and so on. But aside from their property attitude toward other human beings, people experience an unending number of objects, even feelings, as property. Take health and illness, for example. People who discuss their health do so with a proprietary feeling, referring to *their* sicknesses, *their* operations, *their* treatments—*their* diets, *their* medicines. They clearly consider that health and sickness are property; their property relationship to their bad health is analogous, say, to that of a stockholder whose shares are losing part of their original value in a badly falling market.

Ideas and beliefs can also become property, as can even habits. For instance, anyone who eats an identical breakfast at the same time each morning can be disturbed by even a slight change in that routine, because his habit has become a property whose loss endangers his security.

The picture of the universality of the having mode of existence may strike many readers as too negative and one-sided; and indeed it is. I wanted to portray the socially prevalent attitude first in order to give as clear a picture as possible. But there is another element that can give this picture a degree of balance, and that is a growing attitude among the young generation that is quite different from the majority. Among these young people we find patterns of consumption that are not hidden forms of acquisition and having, but expressions of genuine joy in doing what one likes to do without expecting anything "lasting" in return. These young people travel long distances, often with hardships, to hear music they like, to see a place they want to see, to meet people they want to meet. Whether their aims are as valuable as they think they are is not the question here; even if they are without sufficient seriousness, preparation, or concentration, these young people dare to *be*, and they are not interested in what they get in return or what they can keep. They also seem much more sincere than the older generation, although often philosophically and politically naive. They do not polish their egos all the time in order to be a desirable "object" on the market. They do not protect their image by constantly lying, with or without knowing it; they do not expend their energy in repressing truth, as the majority does. And frequently, they impress their elders by their honesty—for their elders secretly admire people who can see and tell the truth. Among them are politically and religiously oriented groups of all shadings, but also many without any particular ideology or doctrine who may say of themselves that they are just "searching." While they may not have found themselves, or a goal that gives guidance to the practice of life, they are searching to be themselves instead of having and consuming.

This positive element in the picture needs to be qualified, however. Many of these same young people (and their number has been markedly decreasing since the late sixties) had not progressed from freedom *from* to freedom *to;* they simply rebelled without attempting to find a goal toward which to move, except that of freedom from restrictions and dependence. Like that of their bourgeois parents, their motto was "New is beautiful!" and they developed an almost phobic disinterest in all tradition, including the thoughts that the greatest minds have produced. In a kind of naïve narcissism they believed that they could discover by themselves all that is worth discovering. Basically, their ideal was to become small children again, and such authors as Marcuse produced the convenient ideology that return to childhood—not development to maturity—is the ultimate goal of socialism and revolution. They were happy as long as they were young enough for this euphoria to last; but many of them have passed this period with severe disappointment, without having acquired well-founded convictions, without a center within themselves. They often end up as disappointed, apathetic persons—or as unhappy fanatics of destruction.

Not all who had started with great hopes ended up with disappointment, however, but it is unfortunately impossible to know what their number is. To my knowledge, no valid statistical data or sound estimates are available, and even if they were available, it is almost impossible to be sure how to qualify the individuals. Today, millions of people in America and Europe try to find contact with tradition and with teachers who can show them the way. But in large part the doctrines and teachers are either fraudulent, or vitiated by the spirit of public relations ballyhoo, or mixed up with the financial and prestige interests of the respective gurus. Some people may genuinely benefit from such mehods in spite of the sham; others will apply them without any serious intention of inner change. But only a detailed quantitative and qualitative analysis of the new believers could show how many belong to each group.

My personal estimate is that the young people (and some older ones) who are seriously concerned with changing from the having to the being mode number more than a few dispersed individuals. I believe that quite a large number of groups and individuals are moving in the direction of being, that they represent a new trend transcending the having orientation of the majority, and that they are of historical significance. It will not be the first time in history that a minority indicates the course that historical development will take. The existence of this minority gives hope for the general change in attitude from having to being. This hope is all the more real since some of the factors that made it possible for these new attitudes to emerge are historical changes that can hardly be reversed: the breakdown of patriarchal supremacy over women and of parents' domination of the young. While the political revolution of the twentieth century, the Russian revolution, has failed (it is too early to judge the final outcome of the Chinese revolution), the victorious revolutions of our century, even though they are only in their first stages, are the women's, the children's, and the sexual revolutions. Their principles have already been accepted by the consciousness of a great many individuals, and every day the old ideologies become more ridiculous.

The Nature of Having

The nature of the having mode of existence follows from the nature of private property. In this mode of existence all that matters is my acquisition of property and my unlimited right to keep what I have acquired. The having mode excludes others; it does not require any further effort on my part to keep my property or to make productive use of it. The Buddha has described this mode of behavior as craving, the Jewish and Christian religions as coveting; it transforms everybody and everything into something dead and subject to another's power.

The sentence "I have something" expresses the relation between the subject, *I* (or he, we, you, they), and the object, *O*. It implies that the subject is permanent and the object is permanent. But is there permanence in the subject? Or in the object? I shall die; I may lose the social position that guarantees my having something. The object is similarly not permanent: it can be destroyed, or it can be lost, or it can lose its value. Speaking of having something permanently rests upon the illusion of a permanent and indestructible substance. If I seem to have everything, I have—in reality—nothing, since my having, possessing, controlling an object is only a transitory moment in the process of living.

In the last analysis, the statement "*I* [subject] have *O* [object]" expresses a definition of *I* through my possession of *O*. The subject is not *myself* but *I am what I have*. My property constitutes myself and my identity. The underlying thought in the statement "I am I" is "*I am I because I have X*"—*X* equaling all natural objects and persons to whom I relate myself through my power to control them, to make them permanently mine.

In the having mode, there is no alive relationship between me and what I have. It and I have become things, and I have *it*, because I have the force to make it mine. But there is also a reverse relationship: *it has me*, because my sense of identity, i.e., of sanity, rests upon my having *it* (and as many things as possible). The having mode of existence is not established by an alive, productive process between subject and object; it makes *things* of both object and subject. The relationship is one of deadness, not aliveness.

Having—Force—Rebellion

The tendency to grow in terms of their own nature is common to all living beings. Hence we resist any attempt to prevent our growing in the ways determined by our structure. In order to break this resistance, whether it is conscious or not, physical or mental force is necessary. Inanimate objects resist control of their physical composition in various degrees through the energy inherent in their atomic and molecular structures. But they do not fight against being used. The use of heteronomous force with living beings (i.e., the force that tends to bend us in directions contrary to our given structure and that is detrimental to our growth) arouses resistance. This resistance can take all forms, from overt, effective, direct, active resistance to indirect, ineffectual, and, very often, unconscious resistance.

What is restricted is the free, spontaneous expression of

the infant's, the child's, the adolescent's, and eventually
the adult's will, their thirst for knowledge and truth, their
wish for affection. The growing person is forced to give
up most of his or her autonomous, genuine desires and
interests, and his or her own will, and to adopt a will and
desires and feelings that are not autonomous but super-
imposed by the social patterns of thought and feeling.
Society, and the family as its psychosocial agent, has to
solve a difficult problem: *How to break a person's will
without his being aware of it?* Yet by a complicated
process of indoctrination, rewards, punishments, and fitting ideology, it solves this task by and large so well that
most people believe they are following their own will and
are unaware that their will itself is conditioned and manipulated.

The greatest difficulty in this suppression of the will
exists with regard to sexuality, because we deal here with
a strong tendency of the natural order that is less easy to
manipulate than many other desires. For this reason society tries harder to fight sexual desires than almost any
other human desire. No need to cite the various forms of
the vilifications of sex from moral grounds (its evilness)
to health grounds (masturbation does physical harm).
The church forbids birth control, not really because of
her concern for the sacredness of life (a concern which
would lead to the condemnation of the death penalty and
of war), but in order to denigrate sex unless it serves
procreation.

The effort made to suppress sex would be difficult to
understand if it were for the sake of sex as such. Not sex,
however, but the breaking of human will is the reason
for vilifying sex. A great number of the so-called primitive societies have no sex tabu whatever. Since they function without exploitation and domination, they do not
have to break the individual's will. They can afford not to
stigmatize sex and to enjoy the pleasure of sexual relations without guilt feelings. Most remarkable in these
societies is that this sexual freedom does not lead to
sexual greed; that after a period of relatively transient
sexual relations couples find each other; that they then
have no desire to swap partners, but are also free to

separate when love has gone. For these not-property-oriented groups sexual enjoyment is an expression of being, not the result of sexual possessiveness. In saying this I do not imply that we should return to living as these primitive societies do—not that we could, even if we wanted to, for the simple reason that the process of individuation and individual differentiation and distance that civilization has brought about gives individual love a different quality from that in primitive society. We cannot regress; we can only move forward. What matters is that new forms of propertylessness will do away with the sexual greed that is characteristic of all having societies.

Sexual desire is one expression of independence that is expressed very early in life (masturbation). Its denunciation serves to break the will of the child and make it feel guilty, and thus more submissive. To a large extent the impulse to break sexual tabus is essentially an attempt at rebellion aimed at restoring one's freedom. But the breaking of sexual tabus as such does not lead to greater freedom; the rebellion is drowned, as it were, in the sexual satisfaction . . . and in the person's subsequent guilt feeling. Only the achievement of inner independence is conducive to freedom and ends the need for fruitless rebellion. The same holds true for all other behavior that aims at doing the forbidden as an attempt to restore one's freedom. *Indeed, tabus create sexual obsessiveness and perversions, but sexual obsessiveness and perversions do not create freedom.*

The rebellion of the child manifests itself in many other ways: by the child's not accepting the rules of cleanliness training; by not eating, or by overeating; by aggression and sadism, and by many kinds of self-destructive acts. Often the rebellion manifests itself in a kind of general "slow-down strike"—a withdrawal of interest in the world, laziness, passivity, up to the most pathological forms of slow self-destruction. The effects of this power struggle between children and parents is the subject of David E. Schecter's paper on "Infant Development." All data indicate that *heteronomous interference with the child's and the later person's growth process is the deep-*

est root of mental pathology, especially of destructiveness.

It must be clearly understood, though, that freedom is not laissez-faire and arbitrariness. Human beings have a specific structure—like any other species—and can grow only in terms of this structure. Freedom does not mean freedom *from* all guiding principles. It means the freedom *to grow* according to the laws of the structure of human existence (autonomous restrictions). It means obedience to the laws that govern optimal human development. Any authority that furthers this goal is "rational authority" when this furtherance is achieved by way of helping to mobilize the child's activity, critical thinking, and faith in life. It is "irrational authority" when it imposes on the child heteronomous norms that serve the purposes of the authority, but not the purposes of the child's specific structure.

The having mode of existence, the attitude centered on property and profit, necessarily produces the desire—indeed the need—for power. To control other living human beings we need to use power to break their resistance. To maintain control over private property we need to use power to protect it from those who would take it from us because they, like us, can never have enough; the desire to have private property produces the desire to use violence in order to rob others in overt or covert ways. In the having mode, one's happiness lies in one's superiority over others, in one's power, and in the last analysis, in one's capacity to conquer, rob, kill. In the being mode it lies in loving, sharing, giving.

Other Factors Supporting the Having Mode

Language is an important factor in fortifying the having orientation. The name of a person—and we all have names (and maybe numbers if the present-day trend toward depersonalization continues)—creates the illusion that he or she is an immortal being. The person and the name become equivalent; the name demonstrates that the person is a lasting, indestructible substance—and not a process. Some nouns have the same function: i.e., love, pride, hate, joy, give the appearance of fixed substances, but such nouns have no reality and only obscure the insight that we are dealing with processes going on in a human being. But even nouns that are names of *things*, such as "table" or "lamp," are misleading. The words indicate that we are speaking of fixed substances, although things are nothing but a process of energy that causes certain sensations in our bodily system. But these sensations are not *perceptions* of specific things like table or lamp; these perceptions are the result of a cultural process of learning, a process that makes certain sensations assume the form of specific percepts. We naively believe that things like tables and lamps exist as such, and we fail to see that society teaches us to transform sensations into perceptions that permit us to manipulate the world around us in order to enable us to survive in a given culture. Once we have given such percepts a name, the name seems to guarantee the final and unchangeable reality of the percept.

The need to have has still another foundation, the *biologically given desire to live*. Whether we are happy or unhappy, our body impels us to strive for *immortality*. But since we know by experience that we shall die, we seek for solutions that make us believe that, in spite of the empirical evidence, we are immortal. This wish has taken many forms: the belief of the Pharaohs that their bodies enshrined in the pyramids would be immortal; many religious fantasies of life after death, in the happy hunting grounds of hunter societies; the Christian and Islam paradise. In contemporary society since the eighteenth century, "history" and "the future" have become the substitutes for the Christian heaven: fame, celebrity, even notoriety—anything that seems to guarantee a footnote in the record of history—constitutes a bit of immortality. The craving for fame is not just secular vanity—it has a religious equality for those who do not believe in the traditional hereafter any more. (This is particularly noticeable among political leaders.) Publicity paves the way to immortality, and the public relations agents become the new priests.

But perhaps more than anything else, possession of property constitutes the fulfillment of the craving for immortality, and it is for this reason that the having orientation has such strength. If my *self* is constituted by what I *have,* then I am immortal if the things I have are indestructible. From Ancient Egypt to today—from physical immortality, via mummification of the body, to legal immortality, via the last will—people have remained alive beyond their physical/mental life-times. Via the legal power of the last will the disposal of our property is determined for generations to come; through the laws of inheritance, I—inasmuch as I am an owner of capital—become immortal.

The Having Mode and the Anal Character

A helpful approach to understanding the mode of having is to recall one of Freud's most significant findings, that after going through their infant phase of mere passive receptivity followed by a phase of aggressive exploitative receptivity, all children, before they reach maturity, go through a phase Freud designated the *anal-erotic.* Freud discovered that this phase often remains dominant during a person's development, and that when it does it leads to the development of the *anal character,* i.e., the character of a person whose main energy in life is directed toward having, saving, and hoarding money and material things as well as feelings, gestures, words, energy. It is the character of the stingy individual and is usually connected with such other traits as orderliness, punctuality, stubbornness, each to a more than ordinary degree. An important aspect of Freud's concept is the symbolic connection between money and feces—gold and dirt—of which he quotes a number of examples. His concept of the anal character as one that has not reached maturity is in fact a sharp criticism of bourgeois society of the nineteenth century, in which the qualities of the anal character constituted the norm for moral behavior and were looked upon as the expression of "human nature." Freud's equation: money $=$ feces is an implicit, although not intended, criticism of the functioning of bourgeois society and its possessiveness and may be compared with Marx's discussion of money in the *Economic and Philosophical Manuscripts*.

It is of little importance in this context that Freud believed that a special phase of the libido development was primary and that the character formation was secondary (while in my opinion it is the product of the interpersonal constellation in one's early life and, most of all, the social conditions conducive to its formation). What matters is Freud's view that *the predominant orientation in possession occurs in the period before the achievement of full maturity and is pathological if it remains permanent*. For Freud, in other words, the person exclusively concerned with having and possession is a neurotic, mentally sick person; hence it would follow that the society in which most of the members are anal characters is a sick society.

Asceticism and Equality

Much of the moral and political discussion has centered on the question: To have or not to have? On the moral-religious level this meant the alternative between the ascetic life and the nonascetic life, the latter including both productive enjoyment and unlimited pleasure. This alternative loses most of its meaning if one's emphasis is not on the single act of behavior but on the attitude underlying it. Ascetic behavior, with its constant preoccupation with nonenjoyment, may be only the negation of strong desires for having and consuming. In the ascetic these desires can be repressed, yet in the very attempt to suppress having and consuming, the person may be equally preoccupied with having and consuming. This denial by over-compensation is, as psychoanalytic data show, very frequent. It occurs in such cases as fanatical vegetarians repressing destructive impulses, fanatical antiabortionists repressing their murderous impulses, fanatics of "virtue" repressing their own "sinful" impulses. What matters here is not a certain conviction as such, but the fanaticism that supports it. This, like all fanaticism, suggests the suspicion that it serves to cover other, and usually the opposite, impulses.

In the economic and political field a similar erroneous alternative is between unrestricted inequality and absolute equality of income. If everybody's possessions are functional and personal, then whether someone has somewhat more than another person does not constitute a social problem, for since possession is not essential, envy does not grow. On the other hand, those who are concerned with equality in the sense that each one's share must be exactly equal to anyone else's show that their own having orientation is as strong as ever, except that it is denied by their preoccupation with exact equality. Behind this concern their real motivation is visible: envy. Those demanding that nobody should have more than themselves are thus protecting themselves from the envy they would feel if anyone had even an ounce more of anything. What matters is that both luxury and poverty shall be eradicated; equality must not mean the quantitative equality of each morsel of material goods, but that income is not differentiated to a point that creates different experiences of life for different groups. In the *Economic and Philosophical Manuscripts* Marx pointed this out in what he calls "crude communism," which "negates the personality of man in every sphere"; this type of communism "is only the culmination of such envy and leveling-down on the basis of a preconceived minimum."

Existential Having

In order to fully appreciate the mode of having that we are dealing with here, yet another qualification seems necessary, that of the function of *existential having;* human existence requires that we have, keep, take care of, and use certain things in order to survive. This holds true for our bodies, for food, shelter, clothing, and for the tools necessary to produce our needs. This form of having may be called existential having because it is rooted in human existence. It is a rationally directed impulse in the pursuit of staying alive—in contrast to the *characterological hav-*

ing we have been dealing with so far, which is a passionate drive to retain and keep that is not innate, but that has developed as the result of the impact of social conditions on the human species as it is biologically given.

Existential having is not in conflict with being; characterological having necessarily is. Even the "just" and the "saintly," inasmuch as they are human, must want to have in the existential sense—while the average person wants to have in the existential *and* in the characterological sense. (See the earlier discussion of existential and characterological dichotomies in *Man for Himself.*)

V

WHAT IS THE BEING MODE?

Most of us know more about the mode of having than we do about the mode of being, because having is by far the more frequently experienced mode in our culture. But something more important than that makes defining the mode of being so much more difficult than defining the mode of having, namely the very nature of the difference between these two modes of existence.

Having refers to *things* and things are fixed and *describable*. Being refers to *experience,* and human experience is in principle not describable. What is fully describable is our *persona*—the mask we each wear, the ego we present—for this persona is in itself a thing. In contrast, the living human being is not a dead image and cannot be described like a thing. In fact, the living human being cannot be described at all. Indeed, much can be said about me, about my character, about my total orientation to life. This insightful knowledge can go very far in understanding and describing my own or another's psychical structure. But the total me, my whole individuality, my suchness that is as unique as my fingerprints are, can never be fully understood, not even by empathy, for no two human beings are identical.* Only in the process of

---

*This is the limitation of even the best psychology, a point I have discussed in detail, comparing "negative psychology" and "negative theology" in an essay. "On the Limitations and Dangers of Psychology" (1959).

mutual alive relatedness can the other and I overcome the barrier of separateness, inasmuch as we both participate in the dance of life. Yet our full identification with each other can never be achieved.

Even a single act of behavior cannot be fully described. One could write pages of description of the Mona Lisa's smile, and still the pictured smile would not have been caught in words—but not because her smile is so "mysterious." Everybody's smile is mysterious (unless it is the learned, synthetic smile of the marketplace). No one can fully describe the expression of interest, enthusiasm, biophilia, or of hate or narcissism that one may see in the eyes of another person, or the variety of facial expressions, of gaits, of postures, of intonations that characterize people.

Being Active

The mode of being has as its prerequisites independence, freedom, and the presence of critical reason. Its fundamental characteristic is that of being active, not in the sense of outward activity, of busyness, but of inner activity, the productive use of our human powers. To be active means to give expression to one's faculties, talents, to the wealth of human gifts with which—though in varying degrees—every human being is endowed. It means to renew oneself, to grow, to flow out, to love, to transcend the prison of one's isolated ego, to be interested, to "list," to give. Yet none of these experiences can be fully expressed in words. The words are vessels that are filled with experience that overflows the vessels. The words point to an experience; they are not the experience. The moment that I express what I experience exclusively in thought and words, the experience has gone: it has dried up, is dead, a mere thought. Hence being is indescribable in words and is communicable only by sharing my experience. In the structure of having, the dead word rules; in the structure of being, the alive and inexpressible experience rules. (Of course, in the being mode there is also thinking that is alive and productive.)

Perhaps the being mode may best be described in a symbol suggested to me by Max Hunziger: A blue glass appears to be blue when light shines through it because it absorbs all other colors and thus does not let them pass. This is to say, we call a glass "blue" precisely because it does not retain the blue waves. It is named not for what it possesses but for what it gives out.

Only to the extent that we decrease the mode of having, that is of nonbeing—i.e., stop finding security and identity by clinging to what we have, by "sitting on it," by holding onto our ego and our possessions—can the mode of being emerge. "To be" requires giving up one's egocentricity and selfishness, or in words often used by the mystics, by making oneself "empty" and "poor."

But most people find giving up their having orientation too difficult; any attempt to do so arouses their intense anxiety and feels like giving up all security, like being thrown into the ocean when one does not know how to swim. They do not know that when they have given up the crutch of property, they can begin to use their own proper forces and walk by themselves. What holds them back is the illusion that they could not walk by themselves, that they would collapse if they were not supported by the things they have.

Activity and Passivity

Being, in the sense we have described it, implies the faculty of being active; passivity excludes being. However, "active" and "passive" are among the most misunderstood words, because their meaning is completely different today from what it was from classic antiquity and the Middle Ages to the period beginning with the Renaissance. In order to understand the concept of being, the concept of activity and passivity must be clarified.

In modern usage activity is usually defined as a quality of behavior that brings about a visible effect by expenditure of energy. Thus, for instance, farmers who cultivate their lands are called active; so are workers on assembly lines, salespeople who persuade their customers to buy, investors who invest their own or other people's money, physicians who treat their patients, clerks who sell postage stamps, bureaucrats who file papers. While some of these activities may require more interest and concentration than others, this does not matter with regard to "activity." Activity, by and large, is *socially recognized purposeful behavior that results in corresponding socially useful changes.*

Activity in the modern sense refers only to *behavior,* not to the person behind the behavior. It makes no difference whether people are active because they are driven by external force, like a slave, or by internal compulsion, like a person driven by anxiety. It does not matter whether they are interested in their work, like a carpenter or a creative writer, or a scientist or a gardener; or whether they have no inner relation to and satisfaction in what they are doing, like the worker on the assembly line or the postal clerk.

The modern sense of activity makes no distinction between *activity* and mere *busyness.* But there is a fundamental difference between the two that corresponds to the terms "alienated" and "nonalienated" in respect to activities. In alienated activity I do not experience myself as the acting subject of my activity; rather, I experience the *outcome* of my activity—and that as something "over there," separated from me and standing above and against me. In alienated activity *I* do not really act; I am *acted upon* by external or internal forces. I have become separated from the result of my activity. The best observable case of alienated activity in the field of psychopathology is that of compulsive-obsessional persons. Forced by an inner urge to do something against their own wills—such as counting steps, repeating certain phrases, performing certain private rituals—they can be extremely active in the pursuit of this aim; but as psychoanalytic investigation has amply shown, they are driven by an inner force that they are unaware of. An equally clear example of alienated activity is posthypnotic behavior. Persons under hypnotic suggestion to do this or that upon awakening from the hypnotic trance will do these things without any awareness that they are not doing what they *want* to do, but are following their respective hypnotists' previously given orders.

In nonalienated activity, I experience *myself* as the *subject* of my activity. Nonalienated activity is a process of giving birth to something, of producing something and remaining related to what I produce. This also implies that my activity is a manifestation of my powers, that I and my activity are one. I call this nonalienated activity *productive activity.**

"Productive" as used here does not refer to the capacity to create something new or original, as an artist or scientist may be creative. Neither does it refer to the product of my activity, but to its *quality*. A painting or a scientific treatise may be quite unproductive, i.e., sterile; on the other hand, the process going on in persons who are aware of themselves in depth, or who truly "see" a tree rather than just look at it, or who read a poem and experience in themselves the movement of feelings the poet has expressed in words—that process may be very productive, although nothing is "produced." Productive activity denotes the state of inner activity; it does not necessarily have a connection with the creation of a work of art, of science, or of something "useful." Productiveness is a character orientation all human beings are capable of, to the extent that they are not emotionally crippled. Productive persons animate whatever they touch. They give birth to their own faculties and bring life to other persons and to things.

"Activity" and "passivity" can each have two entirely different meanings. Alienated activity, in the sense of mere busyness, is actually "passivity," in the sense of productivity; while passivity, in terms of nonbusyness, may be nonalienated activity. This is so difficult to understand today because most activity is alienated "passivity," while productive passivity is rarely experienced.

---

*I used the terms "spontaneous activity" in *Escape from Freedom* and "productive activity" in my later writings.

Activity—Passivity, According to the Masters of Thought

"Activity" and "passivity" were not used in the current sense in the philosophical tradition of preindustrial society. They hardly could have been, since the alienation of work had not reached a point comparable to the one existing now. For this reason such philosophers as *Aristotle* do not even make a clear-cut distinction between "activity" and mere "busyness." In Athens, alienated work was done only by slaves; work which involved bodily labor seems to have been excluded from the concept of *praxis* ("practice"), a term that refers only to almost any kind of activity a *free* person is likely to perform, and essentially the term Aristotle used for a person's free activity. (See Nicholas Lobkowicz, *Theory and Practice.*) Considering this background, the problem of subjectively meaningless, alienated, purely routinized work could hardly arise for free Athenians. Their freedom implied precisely that because they were not slaves, their activity was productive and meaningful to them.

That Aristotle did not share our present concepts of activity and passivity becomes unmistakably clear if we will consider that for him the highest form of praxis, i.e., of activity—even above political activity—is the *contemplative life,* devoted to the search for truth. The idea that contemplation was a form of inactivity was unthinkable for him. Aristotle considers contemplative life the *activity* of the best part in us, the *nous.* The slave can enjoy sensuous pleasure, even as the free do. But *eudaimonia,* "well-being," consists not in pleasures but in *activities in accordance with virtue* (*Nichomachean Ethics,* 1177a, 2 ff.).

Like Aristotle's, *Thomas Aquinas'* position is also in contrast to the modern concept of activity. For Aquinas, too, the life devoted to inner stillness and spiritual knowledge, the *vita contemplativa,* is the highest form of human activity. He concedes that the daily life, the *vita activa,* of the average person, is also valuable, and it leads well-being (*beatitudo*), provided—and this qualification is crucial—that the aim toward which all one's activities are directed is well-being and that one is able to control one's passions and one's body (Thomas Aquinas, *Summa,* 2–2:182, 183; 1–2:4,6).

While Aquinas' attitude is one of a certain compromise, the author of *The Cloud of Unknowing,* a contemporary of *Master Eckhart,* argues sharply against the value of the active life, while Eckhart, on the other hand, speaks out very much in favor of it. The contradiction is not as sharp as it may appear, however, because all agree that activity is "wholesome" only when it is rooted in and expresses the ultimate ethical and spiritual demands. For this reason, for all these teachers, busyness, i.e., activity separated from people's spiritual ground, is to be rejected.*

As a person and as a thinker *Spinoza* embodied the spirit and the values that were alive in Eckhart's time, roughly four centuries earlier; yet he also keenly observed the changes that had occurred in society and in the average person. He was the founder of modern scientific psychology; one of the discoverers of the dimension of the unconscious, and with this enriched insight he gave a more systematic and precise analysis of the difference between activity and passivity than had any of his predecessors.

In his *Ethics,* Spinoza distinguishes between activity and passivity (to act and to suffer) as the two fundamental aspects of the mind's operation. The first criterion for *acting* is that an action follows from human nature: "I say that we act when anything is done, either within us or without us, of which we are the adequate cause, that is to say, when from our nature anything follows, either within or without us, which by that nature alone can be clearly and distinctly understood. On the other hand I say that we suffer [i.e., in Spinoza's sense, are passive] when anything is done within us, or when anything follows from

---

*The writings of W. Lange, N. Lobkowicz, and D. Mieth (1971) can provide further insights into this problem of contemplative life and active life.

our nature of which we are not the cause except partially" (*Ethics*, 3, def. 2).

These sentences are difficult for the modern reader, who is accustomed to think that the term "human nature" does not correspond to any demonstrable empirical data. But for Spinoza, as for Aristotle, this is not so; nor is it for some contemporary neurophysiologists, biologists, and psychologists. Spinoza believes that human nature is as characteristic for human beings as horse nature is for the horse; furthermore, that goodness or badness, success or failure, well-being or suffering, activity or passivity depend on the degree to which persons succeed in achieving the optimal realization of their species nature. The closer we are to arriving at the model of human nature, the greater are our freedom and our well-being.

In Spinoza's model of human beings the attribute of activity is inseparable from another: reason. Inasmuch as we act in accordance with the conditions of our existence, and are aware of these conditions as real and necessary ones, we know the truth about ourselves. "Our mind acts at times and at times suffers: in so far as it has adequate ideas, it necessarily acts: and in so far as it has inadequate ideas, it necessarily suffers" (*Ethics*, 3, prop. 1).

Desires are divided into active and passive ones (*actiones* and *passiones*). The former are rooted in the conditions of our existence (the natural and not the pathological distortions), and the latter are not thus rooted but are caused by inner or outer distorting conditions. The former exist to the extent that we are free; the latter are caused by inner or outer force. All "active affects" are necessarily good: "passions" can be good or evil. According to Spinoza, activity, reason, freedom, well-being, joy, and self-perfection are inseparably connected—in the same way as passivity, irrationality, bondage, sadness, powerlessness, and strivings contrary to the demands of human nature are (*Ethics*, 4, app. 2, 3, 5; props. 40, 42).

One understands Spinoza's ideas about passions and passivity fully only if one proceeds to the last—and most modern—step of his thinking: that to be driven by irrational passions is to be mentally sick. To the degree that we achieve optimal growth, we are not only (relatively) free, strong, rational, and joyous but also mentally healthy; to the degree that we fail to reach this aim, we are unfree, weak, lacking rationality, and depressed. Spinoza, to my knowledge, was the first modern thinker to postulate that mental health and sickness are outcomes of right and wrong living respectively.

For Spinoza mental health is, in the last analysis, a manifestation of right living; mental illness, a symptom of the failure to live according to the requirements of human nature. "But if the *greedy* person thinks only of money and possessions, the ambitious one only of fame, one does not think of them as being insane, but only as annoying; generally one has contempt for them. But *factually*, greediness, ambition, and so forth are forms of insanity, although usually one does not think of them as 'illness' " (*Ethics*, 4, prop. 44). In this statement, so foreign to the thinking of our time, Spinoza considers passions that do not correspond to the needs of human nature as pathological; in fact, he goes so far as to call them a form of insanity.

Spinoza's concepts of activity and passivity are a most radical critique of industrial society. In contrast to today's belief that persons driven mainly by greed for money, possession, or fame are normal and well adjusted, they are considered by Spinoza utterly passive and basically sick. The active persons in Spinoza's sense, which he personified in his own life, have become exceptions, and are somewhat suspected of being "neurotic" because they are so little adapted to so-called normal activity.

Marx wrote (in the *Economic and Philosophical Manuscripts*) that "free conscious activity" (i.e., human activity) is "the species character of man." Labor, for him, represents human activity, and human activity is life. Capital, on the other hand, represents for Marx the amassed, the past, and in the last analysis, the dead (*Grundrisse*). One cannot fully understand the affective charge which the struggle between capital and labor had for Marx unless one considers that for him it was the fight between aliveness and deadness, the present versus the past, people versus things, being versus having. For Marx the question was: Who should rule whom—should life rule the dead, or the dead rule life? Socialism, for him, represented a society in which life had won over the dead.

Marx's whole critique of capitalism and his vision of socialism are rooted in the concept that human self-activity is paralyzed in the capitalist system and that the goal is to restore full humanity by restoring activity in all spheres of life.

Despite the formulations influenced by the classic economists, the cliché that Marx was a determinist, making human beings the passive objects of history and depriving them of their activity, is the very opposite of his thinking, as any who themselves read Marx, rather than a few isolated sentences taken out of context, will be easily convinced. Marx's views could not be more clearly expressed than they are in his own statement: "History does nothing; it possesses no colossal riches, it 'fights no fight.' It is rather man—real, living man—who acts, possesses and fights everything. It is by no means 'History' which uses man as a means to carry out its ends as if it were a person apart; rather History is nothing but the activity of man in pursuit of his ends" (Marx and Engels, *The Holy Family*).

Of near contemporaries none has perceived the passive character of modern activity as penetratingly as has *Albert Schweitzer,* who, in his study of the decay and restoration of civilization, saw modern Man as unfree, incomplete, unconcentrated, pathologically dependent, and "absolutely passive."

Being as Reality

Thus far I have described the meaning of being by contrasting it to having. But a second, equally important meaning of being is revealed by contrasting it to *appearing*. If I appear to be kind while my kindness is only a mask to cover my exploitativeness—if I appear to be courageous while I am extremely vain or perhaps suicidal —if I appear to love my country while I am furthering my selfish interests, the appearance, i.e., my overt behavior, is in drastic contradiction to the reality of forces that motivate me. My behavior is different from my character. My character structure, the true motivation of my behavior, constitutes my real being. My behavior may partly reflect my being, but it is usually a mask that I have and that I wear for my own purposes. Behaviorism deals with this mask as if it were a reliable scientific datum; true insight is focused on the inner reality, which is usually neither conscious nor directly observable. This concept of being as "unmasking," as is expressed by Eckhart, is central in Spinoza's and Marx's thought and is the fundamental discovery of Freud.

To understand the discrepancy between behavior and character, between my mask and the reality it hides, is the main achievement of Freud's psychoanalysis. He devised a method (free association, analysis of dreams, transference, and resistance) that aimed at uncovering the instinctual (essentially sexual) desires that had been repressed in early childhood. Even when later developments in psychoanalytic theory and therapy proceeded to emphasize traumatic events in the field of early interpersonal relations rather than of instinctual life, the principle remained the same: What is repressed are early and—as I believe—later traumatic desires and fears; the way to recovery from symptoms or from a more general malaise lies in uncovering this repressed material. In other words, what is repressed are the irrational, infantile, and individual elements of experience.

On the other hand, the common-sense views of a normal, i.e., socially adapted, citizen were supposed to be rational and not in need of depth analysis. But this is not true at all. Our conscious motivations, ideas, and beliefs are a blend of false information, biases, irrational passions, rationalizations, prejudices, in which morsels of truth swim around and give the reassurance, albeit false, that the whole mixture is real and true. The thinking process attempts to organize this whole cesspool of illusions according to the laws of logic and plausibility. This level of consciousness is supposed to reflect reality; it is the map we use for organizing our life. This false map is not repressed. *What is repressed is the knowledge of reality, the knowledge of what is true.* If we ask, then:

What is unconscious? the answer must be: Aside from irrational passions, almost the whole of knowledge of reality. The unconscious is basically determined by society, which produces irrational passions and provides its members with various kinds of fiction and thus forces the truth to become the prisoner of the alleged rationality.

Stating that the truth is repressed is based, of course, on the premise that we know the truth and repress this knowledge; in other words, that there is "unconscious knowledge." My experience in psychoanalysis—of others and of myself—is that this is indeed true. We perceive reality, and we cannot help perceiving it. Just as our senses are organized to see, hear, smell, touch when we are brought together with reality, our reason is organized to recognize reality, i.e., to see things as they are, to perceive the truth. I am not of course referring to the part of reality that requires scientific tools or methods in order to be perceived. I am referring to what is recognizable by concentrated "seeing," especially the reality in ourselves and in others. We know when we meet a dangerous person, when we meet someobdy we can fully trust; we know when we are lied to, or exploited, or fooled, when we have sold ourselves a bill of goods. We know almost everything that is important to know about human behavior, just as our ancestors had a remarkable knowledge about the movements of the stars. But while they were *aware* of their knowledge and used it, we repress our knowledge immediately, because if it were conscious it would make life too difficult and, as we persuade ourselves, too "dangerous."

The proof of this statement is easy to find. It exists in many dreams in which we exhibit a deep insight into the essence of other people, and of ourselves, which we completely lack in the daytime. (I included examples of "insight dreams" in *The Forgotten Language.*) It is evidenced in those frequent reactions in which we suddenly see somebody in an entirely different light, and then feel as if we had had this knowledge all the time before. It can be found in the phenomenon of resistance when the painful truth threatens to come to the surface: in slips of the tongue, in awkward expressions, in a state of trance, or in instances when a person says something, as if in an aside, that is the very opposite of what he or she always claimed to believe, and then seems to have forgotten this aside a minute later. Indeed, a great deal of our energy is used to hide from ourselves what we know, and the degree of such repressed knowledge can hardly be overestimated. A Talmudic legend has expressed this concept of the repression of the truth, in a poetic form: when a child is born, an angel touches its forehead, so that it forgets the knowledge of the truth that it has at the moment of birth. If the child did not forget, later life would become unbearable.

Returning to our main thesis: Being refers to the real, in contrast to the falsified, illusionary picture. In this sense, any attempt to increase the sector of being means increased insight into the reality of one's self, of others, of the world around us. The main ethical goals of Judaism and Christianity—overcoming greed and hate—cannot be realized without another factor that is central in Buddhism even though it plays also a role in Judaism and in Christianity: The way to being lies in penetrating the surface and grasping reality.

The Will to Give, to Share, to Sacrifice

In contemporary society the having mode of existing is assumed to be rooted in human nature and, hence, virtually unchangeable. The same idea is expressed in the dogma that people are basically lazy, passive by nature, and that they do not want to work or to do anything else, unless they are driven by the incentive of material gain ... or hunger ... or the fear of punishment. This dogma is doubted by hardly anybody, and it determines our methods of education and of work. But it is little more than an expression of the wish to prove the value of our social arrangements by imputing to them that they follow the needs of human nature. To the members of many different societies of both past and present, the concept of innate human selfishness and laziness would appear as fantastic as the reverse sounds to us.

The truth is that both the having and the being modes of existence are potentialities of human nature, that our biological urge for survival tends to further the having mode, but that selfishness and laziness are not the only propensities inherent in human beings.

We human beings have an inherent and deeply rooted desire to be: to express our faculties, to be active, to be related to others, to escape the prison cell of selfishness. The truth of this statement is proven by so much evidence that a whole volume could easily be filled with it. D. O. Hebb has formulated the gist of the problem in the most general form by stating that *the only behavioral problem is to account for inactivity, not for activity.* The following data are evidence for this general thesis:*

1. The data on animal behavior. Experiments and direct observation show that many species undertake difficult tasks with pleasure, even when no material rewards are offered.

2. Neurophysiological experiments demonstrate the activity inherent in the nerve cells.

3. Infantile behavior. Recent studies show the capacity and need of small infants to respond actively to complicated stimuli—findings in contrast to Freud's assumption that the infant experiences the outside stimulus as a threat and that it mobilizes its aggressiveness in order to remove the threat.

4. Learning behavior. Many studies show that the child and adolescent are lazy because learning material is presented to them in a dry and dead way that is incapable of arousing their genuine interest; if the pressure and the boredom are removed and the material is presented in an alive way, remarkable activity and initiative are mobilized.

5. Work behavior. E. Mayo's classic experiment has shown that even work which in itself is boring becomes interesting if the workers know that they are participating in an experiment conducted by an alive and gifted person who has the capacity to arouse their curiosity and their participation.

*I have dealt with some of this evidence in *The Anatomy of Human Destructiveness.*

The same has been shown in a number of factories in Europe and in the United States. The managers' stereotype of the workers is: workers are not really interested in active participation; all they want are higher wages, hence profit sharing might be an incentive for higher work productivity, but not the workers' participation. While the managers are right as far as the work methods they offer are concerned, experience has shown—and has convinced not a few managers—that if the workers can be truly active, responsible, and knowledgeable in their work role, the formerly uninterested ones change considerably and show a remarkable degree of inventiveness, activity, imagination, and satisfaction.*

6. The wealth of data to be found in social and political life. The belief that people do not want to make sacrifices is notoriously wrong. When Churchill announced at the beginning of the Second World War that what he had to demand from the British was blood, sweat, and tears, he did not deter them, but on the contrary, he appealed to their deep-seated human desire to make sacrifices, to give of themselves. The reaction of the British—and of the Germans and the Russians as well—toward the indiscriminate bombing of population centers by the belligerents proves that common suffering did not weaken their spirit; it strengthened their resistance and proved wrong those who believed terror bombing could break the morale of the enemy and help finish the war.

It is a sad commentary on our civilization, however, that war and suffering rather than peacetime living can mobilize human readiness to make sacrifices, and that the

---

*In his forthcoming book *The Gamesmen: The New Corporate Leaders* (which I was privileged to read in manuscript), Michael Maccoby mentions some recent democratic participatory projects, especially his own research in The Bolivar Project. Bolivar is dealt with in the working papers on that project and will be the subject, along with another project, of a larger work that Maccoby is presently planning.

times of peace seem mainly to encourage selfishness. Fortunately, there are situations in peacetime in which human strivings for giving and solidarity manifest themselves in individual behavior. The workers' strikes, especially up to the period of the First World War, are an example of such essentially nonviolent behavior. The workers sought higher wages, but at the same time, they risked and accepted severe hardships in order to fight for their own dignity and the satisfaction of experiencing human solidarity. The strike was as much a "religious" as an economic phenomenon. While such strikes still do occur even today, most present-day strikes are for economic reasons—although strikes for better working conditions have increased recently.

The need to give and to share and the willingness to make sacrifices for others are still to be found among the members of certain professions, such as nurses, physicians, monks, and nuns. The goal of helping and sacrificing is given only lip service by many, if not most, of these professionals; yet the character of a goodly number corresponds to the values they profess. We find the same needs affirmed and expressed in many communes throughout the centuries, whether religious, socialist, or humanist. We find the wish to give in the people who volunteer their blood (without payment), in the many situations in which people risk their lives to save another's. We find the manifestation of the will to give in people who genuinely love. "False love," i.e., shared mutual selfishness, makes people more selfish (and this is the case often enough). Genuine love increases the capacity to love and to give to others. The true lover loves the whole world, in his or her love for a specific person.*

---

*One of the most important sources for understanding the natural human impulse to give and to share is P. A. Kropotkin's classic, *Mutual Aid: A Factor of Evolution* (1902). Two other important works are *The Gift Relationship: From Human Blood to Social Policy* by Richard Titmuss (in which he points to the manifestations of the people's wish to give, and stresses that our economic system prevents people from freely exercising their right to give), and Edmund S. Phelps, ed., *Altruism, Morality and Economic Theory.*

Conversely, we find that not a few people, especially younger ones, cannot stand the luxury and selfishness that surround them in their affluent families. Quite against the expectations of their elders, who think that their children "have everything they wish," they rebel against the deadness and isolation of their lives. For the fact is, they do not have everything they wish and they wish for what they do not have.

Outstanding examples of such people from past history are the sons and daughters of the rich in the Roman Empire, who embraced the religion of poverty and love; and another is the Buddha, who was a prince and had every pleasure and luxury that he could possibly want, but discovered that having and consuming cause unhappiness and suffering. A more recent example (second half of the nineteenth century) is the sons and daughters of the Russian upper class, the *Narodniki*. Finding themselves no longer able to stand the life of idleness and injustice they had been born into, these young people left their families and joined the poor peasants, lived with them, and helped to lay one of the foundationss of the revolutionary struggle in Russia.

We can witness a similar phenomenon among the sons and daughters of the well-to-do in the United States and Germany, who see their life in their affluent home environment as boring and meaningless. But more than that, they find the world's callousness toward the poor and the drift toward nuclear war for the sake of individual egotism unbearable. Thus, they move away from their home environment, looking for a new lifestyle—and remain unsatisfied because no constructive effort seems to have a chance. Many among them were originally the most idealistic and sensitive of the young generation; but at this point, lacking in tradition, maturity, experience, and political wisdom, they become desperate, narcissistically overestimate their own capacities and possibilities, and try to achieve the impossible by the use of force. They form so-called revolutionary groups and expect to save the world by acts of terror and destruction, not seeing that they are only contributing to the general tendency to violence and inhumanity. They have lost their capacity to love and have replaced it with the wish to sacrifice their lives. (Self-sacrifice is frequently the solution for individuals who ardently desire to love, but who have lost the capacity to love and see in the sacrifice of their own lives an experience of love in the highest degree.) But these self-sacrificing young people are very different from the *loving martyrs,* who want to live because they love life and who accept death only when they are forced to die in order not to betray themselves. Our present-day self-sacrificing young people are the accused, but they are also the accusers, in demonstrating that in our social system some of the very best young people become so isolated and hopeless that nothing but destruction and fanaticism are left as a way out of their despair.

The human desire to experience union with others is rooted in the specific conditions of existence that characterize the human species and is one of the strongest motivators of human behavior. By the combination of minimal instinctive determination and maximal development of the capacity for reason, we human beings have lost our original oneness with nature. In order not to feel utterly isolated—which would, in fact, condemn us to insanity—we need to find a new unity: with our fellow beings and with nature. This human need for unity with others is experienced in many ways: in the symbiotic tie to mother, an idol, one's tribe, one's nation, one's class, one's religion, one's fraternity, one's professional organization. Often, of course, these ties overlap, and often they assume an ecstatic form, as among members of certain religious sects or of a lynch mob, or in the outbursts of national hysteria in the case of war. The outbreak of the First World War, for example, occasioned one of the most drastic of these ecstatic forms of "union." Suddenly, from one day to the next, people gave up their lifelong convictions of pacifism, antimilitarism, socialism; scientists threw away their lifelong training in objectivity, critical thinking, and impartiality in order to join the big *We.*

The desire to experience union with others manifests itself in the lowest kind of behavior, i.e., in acts of sadism and destruction, as well as in the highest: solidarity on the basis of an ideal or conviction. It is also the main cause of the need to adapt; human beings are more afraid of being outcasts than even of dying. Crucial to every society is the kind of union and solidarity it fosters and the kind it *can* further, under the given conditions of its socioeconomic structure.

These considerations seem to indicate that both tendencies are present in human beings: the one, to *have*—to possess—that owes its strength in the last analysis to the biological factor of the desire for survival; the other, to *be*—to share, to give, to sacrifice—that owes its strength to the specific conditions of human existence and the inherent need to overcome one's isolation by oneness with others. From these two contradictory strivings in every human being it follows that the social structure, its values and norms, decides which of the two becomes dominant. Cultures that foster the greed for possession, and thus the having mode of existence, are rooted in one human potential; cultures that foster being and sharing are rooted in the other potential. We must decide which of these two potentials we want to cultivate, realizing, however, that our decision is largely determined by the socioeconomic structure of a given society that inclines us toward one or the other solution.

From my observations in the field of group behavior my best guess is that the two extreme groups, respectively manifesting deeply ingrained and almost unalterable types of having and of being, form a small minority; that in the vast majority both possibilities are real, and which of the two becomes dominant and which is repressed depends on environmental factors.

This assumption contradicts a widely held psychoanalytic dogma that environment produces essential changes in personality development in infancy and early childhood, but that after this period the character is fixed and hardly changed by external events. This psychoanalytic dogma has been able to gain acceptance beause the basic conditions of their childhood continue into most people's later life, since in general, the same social conditions continue to exist. But numerous instances exist in which a drastic change in environment leads to a fundamental change in behavior, i.e., when the negative forces cease to be fed and the positive forces are nurtured and encouraged.

To sum up, the frequency and intensity of the desire to share, to give, and to sacrifice are not surprising if we consider the conditions of existence of the human species. What is surprising is that this need could be so repressed as to make acts of selfishness the rule in industrial (and many other) societies and acts of solidarity the exception. But, paradoxically, this very phenomenon is caused by the need for union. A society whose principles are acquisition, profit, and property produces a social character oriented around having, and once the dominant pattern is established, nobody wants to be an outsider, or indeed an outcast; in order to avoid this risk everybody adapts to the majority, who have in common only their mutual antagonism.

As a consequence of the dominant attitude of selfishness, the leaders of our society believe that people can be motivated only by the expectation of material advantages, i.e., by rewards, and that they will not react to appeals for solidarity and sacrifice. Hence, except in times of war, these appeals are rarely made, and the chances to observe the possible results of such appeals are lost.

Only a radically different socioeconomic structure and a radically different picture of human nature could show that bribery is not the only way (or the best way) to influence people.

VI

FURTHER ASPECTS OF HAVING AND BEING

Security—Insecurity

Not to move forward, to stay where we are, to regress, in other words to rely on what we have, is very tempting, for what we *have*, we know; we can hold onto it, feel secure in it. We fear, and consequently avoid, taking a step into the unknown, the uncertain; for, indeed, while the *step* may not appear risky to us *after* we have taken it, *before* we take that step the new aspects beyond it appear very risky, and hence frightening. Only the old, the tried, is safe; or so it seems. Every new step contains the danger of failure, and that is one of the reasons people are so afraid of freedom.*

Naturally, at every state of life "the old and accustomed" is different. As infants we *have* only our body and our mother's breasts (originally still undifferentiated). Then we start to orient ourselves to the world, beginning the process of making a place for ourselves in it. We begin wanting to *have* things: we *have* our mother, father, siblings, toys; later on we *acquire* knowledge, a job, a social position, a spouse, children, and then we *have* a kind of afterlife already, when we acquire a burial plot and life insurance and make our "last will."

*This is the main topic in *Escape from Freedom*.

Yet in spite of the security of having, people admire those with a vision of the new, those who break a new path, who have the courage to move forward. In mythology this mode of existence is represented symbolically by the *hero*. Heroes are those with the courage to leave what they have—their land, their family, their property—and move out, not without fear, but without succumbing to their fear. In the Buddhist tradition the Buddha is the hero who leaves all possessions, all certainty contained in Hindu theology—his rank, his family—and moves on to a life of nonattachment. Abraham and Moses are heroes in the Jewish tradition. The Christian hero is Jesus, who had nothing and—in the eyes of the world—is nothing, yet who acts out of the fullness of his love for all human beings. The Greeks have secular heroes, whose aim is victory, satisfaction of their pride, conquest. Yet, like the spiritual heroes, Hercules and Odysseus move forward, undeterred by the risks and dangers that await them. The fairy tale heroes meet the same criteria: leaving, moving forward, and tolerating uncertainty.

We admire these heroes because we deeply feel their way is the way we would want to be—if we could. But being afraid, we believe that we cannot be that way, that only the heroes can. The heroes become idols; we transfer to them our own capacity to move, and then stay where we are—"because we are not heroes."

This discussion might seem to imply that while being a hero is desirable, it is foolish and against one's self-interest. Not so, by any means. The cautious, the having persons enjoy security, yet by necessity they are very insecure. They depend on what they have: money, prestige, their ego—that is to say, on something outside themselves. But what becomes of them if they lose what they have? For, indeed, whatever one has can be lost. Most obviously, one's property can be lost—and with it usually one's position, one's friends—and at any moment one can, and sooner or later one is bound to, lose one's life.

If I am what I have and if what I have is lost, who then am I? Nobody but a defeated, deflated, pathetic testimony to a wrong way of living. Because I *can* lose what I have, I am necessarily constantly worried that I *shall* lose what I have. I am afraid of thieves, of economic changes, of revolutions, of sickness, of death, and I am afraid of love, of freedom, of growth, of change, of the unknown. Thus I am continuously worried, suffering from a chronic hypochondriasis, with regard not only to loss of health but to any other loss of what I have; I become defensive, hard, suspicious, lonely, driven by the need to have more in order to be better protected. Ibsen has given a beautiful description of this self-centered person in his *Peer Gynt*. The hero is filled only with himself; in his extreme egoism he believes that he is *himself*, because *he* is a "bundle of desires." At the end of his life he recognizes that because of his property-structured existence, he has failed to be himself, that he is like an onion without a kernel, an unfinished man, who never was himself.

The anxiety and insecurity engendered by the danger of losing what one has are absent in the being mode. If *I am who I am* and not what I have, nobody can deprive me of or threaten my security and my sense of identity. My center is within myself; my capacity for being and for expressing my essential powers is part of my character structure and depends on me. This holds true for the normal process of living, not, of course, for such circumstances as incapacitating illness, torture, or other cases of powerful external restrictions.

While having is based on some thing that is diminished by use, being grows by practice. (The "burning bush" that is not consumed is the biblical symbol for this paradox.) The powers of reason, of love, of artistic and intellectual creation, all essential powers grow through the process of being expressed. What is spent is not lost, but on the contrary, what is kept is lost. The only threat to my security in being lies in myself: in lack of faith in life and in my productive powers; in regressive tendencies; in inner laziness and in the willingness to have others take over my life. But these dangers are not *inherent* in being, as the danger of losing is inherent in having.

Solidarity—Antagonism

The experience of loving, liking, enjoying something without wanting to *have* it is the one Suzuki referred to in contrasting the Japanese and the English poems (see Chapter I). It is indeed not easy for modern Western Man to experience enjoyment separate from having. However, neither is it entirely foreign to us. Suzuki's example of the flower would not apply if instead of looking at the flower the wanderer looked at a mountain, a meadow, or anything that cannot be physically taken away. To be sure, many, or most, people would not really *see* the mountain, except as a cliché; instead of *seeing* it they would want to know its name and its height—or they might want to climb it, which can be another form of taking possession of it. But some can genuinely see the mountain and enjoy it. The same may be said in respect to appreciating works of music: that is, buying a recording of music one loves can be an act of possessing the work, and perhaps the majority of people who enjoy art really do "consume" it; but a minority probably still responds to music and art with genuine joy and without any impulse to "have."

Sometimes one can read people's responses in their facial expressions. I recently saw a television film of the extraordinary acrobats and jugglers of the Chinese circus during which the camera repeatedly surveyed the audience, to register the response of individuals in the crowd. Most of the faces were lit up, brought to life, became beautified in response to the graceful, alive performance. Only a minority seemed cold and unmoved.

Another example of enjoying without wanting to possess may be readily seen in our response to small children. Here, too, I suspect a great deal of self-deceptive behavior takes place, for we like to see ourselves in the role of lovers of children. But even though there may be reason for suspicion, I believe that genuine, alive response to infants is not at all rare. This may be partly so because, in contrast to their feelings about adolescents and adults, most people are not afraid of children and so feel free to respond to them lovingly, which we cannot do if fear stands in our way.

The most relevant example for enjoyment without the craving to have what one enjoys may be found in interpersonal relations. A man and a woman may enjoy each other on many grounds; each may like the other's attitudes, tastes, ideas, temperament, or whole personality. Yet only in those who must *have* what they like will this mutual enjoyment habitually result in the desire for sexual possession. For those in a dominant mode of being, the other person is enjoyable, and even erotically attractive, but she or he does not have to be "plucked," to speak in terms of Tennyson's poem, in order to be enjoyed.

Having-centered persons want to *have* the person they like or admire. This can be seen in relations between parents and their children, between teachers and students, and between friends. Neither partner is satisfied simply to enjoy the other person; each wishes to have the other person for him- or herself. Hence, each is jealous of those who also want to "have" the other. Each partner seeks the other like a ship-wrecked sailor seeking a plank—for survival. Predominantly "having" relationships are heavy, burdened, filled with conflicts and jealousies.

Speaking more generally, the fundamental elements in the relation between individuals in the having mode of existence are competition, antagonism, and fear. The antagonistic element in the having relationship stems from its nature. If having is the basis of my sense of identity because "I am what I have," the wish to have must lead to the desire to have much, to have more, to have most. In other words, *greed* is the natural outcome of the having orientation. It can be the greed of the miser or the greed of the profit hunter or the greed of the womanizer or the man chaser. Whatever constitutes their greed, the greedy can never have enough, can never be "satisfied." In contrast to physiological needs, such as hunger, that have definite satiation points due to the physiology of the body, *mental* greed—and all greed is mental, even if it is satisfied via the body—has no satiation point, since its consummation does not fill the inner emptiness, boredom, loneliness, and depression it is meant to overcome. In addition, since what one has can be taken away in one form or another, one must have more, in order to fortify one's existence against such danger. If everyone wants to have more, everyone must fear one's neighbor's aggressive intention to take away what one has. To prevent such attack one must become more powerful and preventively aggressive oneself. Besides, since production, great as it may be, can never keep pace with *unlimited* desires, there must be competition and antagonism among individuals in the struggle for getting the most. And the strife would continue even if a state of absolute abundance could be reached; those who have less in physical health and in attractiveness, in gifts, in talents would bitterly envy those who have "more."

That the having mode and the resulting greed necessarily lead to interpersonal antagonism and strife holds true for nations as it does for individuals. For as long as nations are composed of people whose main motivation is having and greed, they cannot help waging war. They necessarily covet what another nation has, and attempt to get what they want by war, economic pressure, or threats. They will use these procedures against weaker nations, first of all, and form alliances that are stronger than the nation that is to be attacked. Even if it has only a reasonable chance to win, a nation will wage war, not because it suffers economically, but because the desire to have more and to coquer is deeply ingrained in the social character.

Of course there are times of peace. But one must distinguish between lasting peace and peace that is a transitory phenomenon, a period of gathering strength, rebuilding one's industry and army—in other words, between peace that is a permanent state of harmony and peace that is essentially only a truce. While the nineteenth and twentieth centuries had periods of truce, they are characterized by a state of chronic war among the main actors on the historical stage. Peace as a state of lasting harmonious relations between nations is only possible when the having structure is replaced by the being structure. The idea that one can build peace while encouraging the striving for possession and profit is an illusion, and a dangerous one, because it deprives people of recognizing that they are confronted with a clear alternative: either a radical change of their character or the perpetuity of war. This is indeed an old alternative; the leaders have chosen war and the people followed them. Today and tomorrow, with the incredible increase in the destructiveness of the new weapons, the alternative is no longer war—but mutual suicide.

What holds true of international wars is equally true for class war. The war between classes, essentially the exploiting and the exploited, has always existed in societies that were based on the principle of greed. There was no class war where there was neither a need for nor a possibility of exploitation. But there are bound to be classes in any society, even the richest, in which the having mode is dominant. As already noted, given unlimited desires, even the greatest production cannot keep pace with everybody's fantasy of having more than their neighbors. Necessarily, those who are stronger, more clever, or more favored by other circumstances will try to establish a favored position for themselves and try to take advantage of those who are less powerful, either by force and violence or by suggestion. Oppressed classes will overthrow their rulers, and so on; the class struggle might perhaps become less violent, but it cannot disappear as long as greed dominates the human heart. The idea of a classless society in a so-called socialist world filled with the spirit of greed is as illusory—and dangerous—as the idea of permanent peace among greedy nations.

In the being mode, private having (private property) has little affective importance, because I do not need to own something in order to enjoy it, or even in order to use it. In the being mode, more than one person—in fact millions of people—can share in the enjoyment of the same object, since none need—or want—to *have* it, as a condition of enjoying it. This not only avoids strife; it creates one of the deepest forms of human happiness: shared enjoyment. Nothing unites people more (without restricting their individuality) than sharing their admiration and love for a person; sharing an idea, a piece of music, a painting, a symbol; sharing in a ritual—and sharing sorrow. The experience of sharing makes and keeps the relation between two individuals alive; it is the basis of all great religious, political, and philosophical movements. Of course, this holds true only as long as and to the extent that the individuals genuinely love or admire. When religious and political movements ossify, when bureaucracy manages the people by means of suggestions and threats, the sharing becomes one of things rather than one of experiences.

While nature has devised, as it were, the prototype—or perhaps the symbol—of shared enjoyment in the sexual act, empirically the sexual act is not necessarily an enjoyment that is shared; the partners are frequently so narcissistic, self-involved, and possessive that one can speak only of simultaneous, but not of shared pleasure.

In another respect, however, nature offers a less ambiguous symbol for the distinction between having and being. The erection of the penis is entirely functional. The male does not *have* an erection, like a property or a permanent quality (although how many men wish to *have* one is anybody's guess). The penis *is* in a state of erection, as long as the man is in a state of excitement, as long as he desires the person who has aroused his excitement. If for one reason or another something interferes with this excitement, the man *has* nothing. And in contrast to practically all other kinds of behavior, the erection cannot be faked. George Groddek, one of the most outstanding, although relatively little known, psychoanalysts, used to comment that a man, after all, is a man for only a few minutes; most of the time he is a little boy. Of course, Groddek did not mean that a man becomes a little boy in his total being, but precisely in that aspect which for many a man is the proof that he is a man. (See the paper I wrote [1943] on "Sex and Character.")

Joy—Pleasure

Master Eckhart taught that aliveness is conducive to *joy*. The modern reader is apt not to pay close attention to the word "joy" and to read it as if Eckhart had written "pleasure." Yet the distinction between joy and pleasure is crucial, particularly so in reference to the distinction between the being and the having modes. It is not easy to appreciate the difference, since we live in a world of "joyless pleasures."

What is pleasure? Even though the word is used in different ways, considering its use in popular thought, it seems best defined as the satisfaction of a desire that does not require activity (in the sense of aliveness) to be satisfied. Such pleasure can be of high intensity: the pleasure in having social success, earning more money, winning a lottery; the conventional sexual pleasure; eating to one's "heart's content"; winning a race; the state of elation brought about by drinking, trance, drugs; the pleasure in satisfying one's sadism, or one's passion to kill or dismember what is alive.

Of course, in order to become rich or famous, individuals must be very active in the sense of busyness, but not in the sense of the "birth within." When they have achieved their goal they may be "thrilled," "intensely satisfied," feel they have reached a "peak." But what peak? Maybe a peak of excitement, of satisfaction, of a trancelike or an orgiastic state. But they may have reached this state driven by passions that, though human, are nevertheless pathological, inasmuch as they do not lead to an intrinsically adequate solution of the human condition. Such passions do not lead to greater human growth and strength but, on the contrary, to human crippling. The pleasures of the radical hedonists, the satisfaction of ever new cupidities, the pleasures of contemporary society produce different degrees of *excitements*. But they are not conducive to *joy*. In fact, the lack of joy makes it necessary to seek ever new, ever more exciting pleasures.

In this respect, modern society is in the same position the Hebrews were in three thousand years ago. Speaking to the people of Israel about one of the worst of their sins, Moses said: "You did not serve the Lord your God with *joy* and *gladness* of heart, in the midst of the fullness of all things" (Deuteronomy 28:47). Joy is the concomitant of productive activity. It is not a "peak experience," which culminates and ends suddenly, but rather a plateau, a feeling state that accompanies the productive expression of one's essential human faculties. Joy is not the ecstatic fire of the moment. Joy is the glow that accompanies being.

Pleasure and thrill are conducive to sadness after the so-called peak has been reached; for the thrill has been experienced, but the vessel has not grown. One's inner powers have not increased. One has made the attempt to break through the boredom of unproductive activity and for a moment has unified all one's energies—except reason and love. One has attempted to become superhuman, without being human. One seems to have succeeded to the moment of triumph, but the triumph is followed by deep sadness: because nothing has changed within oneself. The saying "After intercourse the animal is sad" ("*Post coitum animal triste est*") expresses the same phenomenon with regard to loveless sex, which is a "peak experience" of intense excitation, hence thrilling and pleasureful, and necessarily followed by the disappointment of its ending. Joy in sex is experienced only when physical intimacy is at the same time the intimacy of loving.

As is to be expected, joy must play a central role in those religious and philosophical systems that proclaim *being* as the goal of life. Buddhism, while rejecting pleasure, conceives a state of Nirvana to be a state of joy, which is manifested in the reports and pictures of the Buddha's death. (I am indebted to the late D. T. Suzuki for pointing this out to me in a famous picture of the Buddha's death.)

The Old Testament and the later Jewish tradition, while warning against the pleasures that spring from the satisfaction of cupidity, see in joy the mood that accompanies being. The Book of Psalms ends with the group of fifteen psalms that are one great hymn of joy, and the dynamic psalms begin in fear and sadness and end in joy and gladness.* The Sabbath is the day of joy, and in the Messianic Time joy will be the prevailing mood. The prophetic literature abounds with the expression of joy in

---

*I have analyzed these psalms in *You Shall Be as God*.

such passages as: "Then there will the virgins rejoice in the dance, both young men and old together: for I will turn their mourning into joy" (Jeremiah 31:13) and "With joy you will draw water" (Isaiah 12:3). God calls Jerusalem "the city of my joy" (Jeremiah 49:25).

We find the same emphasis in the Talmud: "The joy of a mitzvah [the fulfillment of a religious duty] is the only way to get the holy spirit" (Berakoth 31, a). Joy is considered so fundamental that, according to Talmudic law, the mourning for a close relative, whose death occurred less than a week earlier, must be interrupted by the joy of Sabbath.

The Hasidic movement, whose motto, "Serve God with joy," was a verse from the psalms, created a form of living in which joy was one of the outstanding elements. Sadness and depression were considered signs of spiritual error, if not outright sin.

In the Christian development even the name of the gospels—*Glad* Tidings—shows the central place of gladness and joy. In the New Testament, joy is the fruit of giving up having, while sadness is the mood of the one who hangs onto possessions. (See, for instance, Matthew 13:44 and 19:22.) In many of Jesus' utterances joy is conceived as a concomitant of living in the mode of being. In his last speech to the Apostles, Jesus tells of joy in the final form: "These things I have spoken to you, that my joy be in you, and that your joy may be full" (John 15:11).

As indicated earlier, joy also plays a supreme role in Master Eckhart's thinking. Here is one of the most beautiful and poetic expressions of the idea of the creative power of laughter and joy: "When God laughs at the soul and the soul laughs back at God, the persons of the Trinity are begotten. To speak in hyperbole, when the Father laughs to the son and the son laughs back to the Father, that laughter gives pleasure, that pleasure gives joy, that joy gives love and love gives the persons [of the Trinity] of which the Holy Spirit is one" (Blakney, p. 245).

Spinoza gives joy a supreme place in his anthropological-ethical system. "Joy," he says, "is man's passage from

a lesser to a greater perfection. *Sorrow* is man's passage
from a greater to a less perfection" (*Ethics*, 3, defs. 2,
3).

Spinoza's statements will be fully understood only if we
put them in the context of his whole system of thought. In
order not to decay, we must strive to approach the "model of human nature," that is, we must be optimally free,
rational, active. We must become what we can be. This is
to be understood as the good that is potentially inherent
in our nature. Spinoza understands "good" as "everything
which we are certain is a means by which we may
approach nearer and nearer to the model of human nature we have set before us"; he understands "evil" as "on
the contrary . . . everything which we are certain hinders
us from reaching that model" (*Ethics*, 4, Preface). Joy is
good; sorrow (*tristitia*, better translated as "sadness,"
"gloom") is bad. Joy is virtue; sadness is sin.

Joy, then, is what we experience in the process of
growing nearer to the goal of becoming ourself.

Sin and Forgiveness

In its classic concept in Jewish and Christian theological thought, sin is essentially identical with *disobedience*
toward the will of God. This is quite apparent in the
commonly held source of the first sin, Adam's disobedience. In the Jewish tradition this act was not understood
as "original" sin that all of Adam's descendants inherited,
as in the Christian tradition, but only as the *first* sin—not
necessarily present in Adam's descendants.

Yet the common element is the view that disobedience
of God's commands *is* sin, whatever the commands are.
This is not surprising if we consider that the image of
God in that part of the biblical story is of a strict
authority, patterned on the role of an Oriental King of
Kings. It is furthermore not surprising if we consider that
the church, almost from its start, adjusted itself to a
social order that, then in feudalism as now in capitalism,
required for its functioning strict obedience of the individuals to the laws, those that serve their true interests as
well as those that do not. How oppressive or how liberal

the laws and what the means for their enforcement are make little difference with regard to the central issue: the people must learn to fear authority, and not only in the person of the "law enforcement" officers bécause they carry weapons. This fear is not enough of a safeguard for the proper functioning of the state; the citizen must internalize this fear and give disobedience a moral and religious quality: sin.

People respect the laws not only because they are afraid but also because they feel guilty for their disobedience. This feeling of guilt can be overcome by the forgiveness that ony the authority itself can grant. The conditions for such forgiveness are: the sinner repents, is punished, and by accepting punishment submits again. The sequence: sin (disobedience) → feeling of guilt → new submission (punishment) → forgiveness, is a vicious circle, inasmuch as each act of disobedience leads to increased obedience. Only a few are not thus cowed. Prometheus is their hero. In spite of the most cruel punishment Zeus afflicts him with, Prometheus does not submit, nor does he feel guilty. He knew that taking the fire away from the gods and giving it to human beings was an act of compassion; he had been disobedient, but he had not sinned. He had, like many other loving heroes (martyrs) of the human race, broken through the equation between disobedience and sin.

Society, though, is not made up of heroes. As long as the tables were set for only a minority, and the majority had to serve the minority's purposes and be satisfied with what was left over, the sense that disobedience is sin had to be cultivated. Both state and church cultivated it, and both worked together, because both had to protect their own hierarchies. The state needed religion to have an ideology that fused disobedience and sin; the church needed believers whom the state had trained in the virtues of obedience. Both used the institution of the family, whose function it was to train the child in obedience from the first moment it showed a will of its own (usually, at the latest, with the beginning of toilet training). The self-will of the child had to be broken in order to prepare it for its proper functioning later on as a citizen.

Sin in the conventional theological and secular sense is a concept within the authoritarian structure, and this structure belongs to the having mode of existence. Our human center does not lie in ourselves, but in the authority to which we submit. We do not arrive at well-being by our own productive activity, but by passive obedience and the ensuing approval by the authority. We *have* a leader (secular or spiritual, king/queen or God) in whom we *have* faith; we *have* security ... as long as we *are*—nobody. That the submission is not necessarily conscious as such, that it can be mild or severe, that the psychic and social structure need not be totally authoritarian, but may be only partially so, must not blind us to the fact that *we live in the mode of having to the degree that we internalize the authoritarian structure of our society*.

As Alfons Auer has emphasized very succinctly, Thomas Aquinas' concept of authority, disobedience, and sin is a humanistic one: i.e., sin is not disobedience of irrational authority, but the violation of human *well-being*.* Thus Aquinas can state: "God can never be insulted by us, except we act against our own well-being" (S.c. gent. 3, 122). To appreciate this position, we must consider that, for Thomas, the human good (*bonum humanum*) is determined neither arbitrarily by purely subjective desires, nor by instinctively given desires ("natural," in the Stoic sense), nor by God's arbitrary will. It is determined by our rational understanding of human nature and of the norms that, based on this nature, are conducive to our optimum growth and well-being. (It should be noted that as an obedient son of the church and a supporter of the existing social order against the revolutionary sects, Thomas Aquinas could not be a pure representative of nonauthoritarian ethic; his use of the word "disobedience" for both kinds of disobedience served to obscure the intrinsic contradiction in his position.)

While sin as disobedience is part of the authoritarian

---

*Professor Auer's yet unpublished paper on the autonomy of ethics according to Thomas Aquinas (which I am indebted to him for letting me read in manuscript) is very helpful to an understanding of Aquinas' ethical concept. So also is his article on the question "Is sin an insult to God?" (See Bibliography.)

and, that is, the *having* structure, it has an entirely different meaning in the nonauthoritarian structure, which is
rooted in the *being* mode. This other meaning, too, is
implied in the biblical story of the Fall and can be
understood by a different interpretation of that story. God
had put Man into the Garden of Eden and warned him
not to eat either from the Tree of Life or from the Tree of
Knowledge of Good and Evil. Seeing that "it was not
good that Man should be alone," God created Woman.
Man and Woman should become one. Both were naked,
and "they were not ashamed." This statement is usually
interpreted in terms of conventional sexual mores, which
assume that, naturally, a man and a woman would be
ashamed if their genitals were uncovered. But this seems
hardly all the text has to say. On a deeper level, this
statement could imply that although Man and Woman
faced each other totally, they did not, and they even
could not, feel ashamed, for they did not experience each
other as strangers, as separated individuals, but as "one."

This prehuman situation changes radically after the
Fall, when Man and Woman become fully human, i.e.,
endowed with reason, with awareness of good and evil,
with awareness of each other as separate beings, with
awareness that their original oneness is broken and that
they have become strangers to one another. They are
close to each other, and yet they feel separate and distant.
They feel the deepest shame there is: the shame of facing
a fellow being "nakedly" and simultaneously experiencing
the mutual estrangement, the unspeakable abyss that separates each from the other. "They made themselves
aprons," thus trying to avoid the full human encounter,
the nakedness in which they see each other. But the
shame, as well as the guilt, cannot be removed by con-
cealment. They did not reach out to each other in love;
perhaps they desired each other physically, but physical
union does not heal human estrangement. That they do
not love each other is indicated in their attitude toward
each other: Eve does not try to protect Adam, and Adam
avoids punishment by denouncing Eve as the culprit rather than defending her.

What is the sin they have committed? To face each

other as separated, isolated, selfish human beings who cannot overcome their separation in the act of loving union. This sin is rooted in our very human existence. Being deprived of the original harmony with nature, characteristic of the animal whose life is determined by built-in instincts, being endowed with reason and self-awareness, we cannot help experiencing our utter separateness from every other human being. In Catholic theology this state of existence, complete separateness and estrangement from each other, not bridged by love, is the definition of "Hell." It is unbearable for us. We must overcome the torture of absolute separateness in some way: by submission or by domination or by trying to silence reason and awareness. Yet all these ways succeed only for the moment, and block the road to a true solution. There is but one way to save ourselves from this hell: to leave the prison of our egocentricity, to reach out and to *one* ourselves with the world. If egocentric separateness is the cardinal sin, then the sin is atoned in the act of loving. The very word "atonement" expresses this concept, for it etymologically derives from "at-*one*ment," the Middle-English expression for union. Since the sin of separateness is not an act of disobedience, it does not need to be *forgiven*. But it does need to be *healed;* and love, not acceptance of punishment, is the healing factor.

Rainer Funk has pointed out to me that the concept of sin as disunion has been expressed by some of the church fathers, who followed Jesus' nonauthoritarian concept of sin, and suggests the following examples (taken from Henri de Lubac): Origines says, "Where there are sins there is diversity. But where virtue rules there is uniqueness, there is oneness." Maximus Confessor says that through Adam's sin the human race, "which should be a harmonious whole without conflict between mine and thine, was transformed into a dust cloud of individuals." Similar thoughts concerning the destruction of the original unity in Adam can also be found in the ideas of St. Augustine and, as Professor Auer points out, in the teaching of Thomas Aquinas. De Lubac says, summing up: "As work of 'restitution' (*Wiederherstellung*), the fact of salvation appears necessary as the regaining of the lost oneness, as the restitution of the supernatural oneness with God and at the same time the oneness of men among each other" (my translation; see also "The Concept of Sin and Repentance" in *You Shall Be as Gods* for an examination of the whole problem of sin).

To sum up, in the having mode, and thus the authoritarian structure, sin is disobedience and is overcome by repentance → punishment → renewed submission. In the being mode, the nonauthoritarian structure, sin is unresolved estrangement, and it is overcome by the full unfolding of reason and love, by at-onement.

One can indeed interpret the story of the Fall in both ways, because the story itself is a blending of authoritarian and liberating elements. But in themselves the concepts of sin as, respectively, disobedience and alienation are diametrically opposed.

The Old Testament story of the Tower of Babel seems to contain the same idea. The human race has reached here a state of union, symbolized by the fact that all humanity has one language. By their own ambition for power, by their craving to *have* the great tower, the people destroy their unity and are disunited. In a sense, the story of the Tower is the second "Fall," the sin of historical humanity. The story is complicated by God's being afraid of the people's unity and the power following from it. "Behold, they are one people, and they have all one language; and this is only the beginning of what they will do, and nothing that they propose to do will now be impossible for them. Come, let us go down and there confuse their language, that they may not understand one another's speech" (Genesis 11:6–7). Of course, the same difficulty already exists in the story of the Fall; there God is afraid of the power that man and woman would exercise if they ate of the fruit of both trees.

Fear of Dying—Affirmation of Living

As stated earlier, the fear that one may lose one's possessions is an unavoidable consequence of a sense of security that is based on what one has. I want to carry this thought a step further.

It may be possible for us not to attach ourselves to *property* and, hence, not fear losing it. But what about the fear of losing life itself—the fear of dying? Is this a fear only of older people or of the sick? Or is everybody afraid of dying? Does the fact that we are bound to die permeate our whole life? Does the fear of dying grow only more intense and more conscious the closer we come to the limits of life by age or sickness?

We have need of large systematic studies by psychoanalysts investigating this phenomenon from childhood to old age and dealing with the unconscious as well as the conscious manifestations of the fear of dying. These studies need not be restricted to individual cases; they could examine large groups, using existing methods of sociopsychoanalysis. Since such studies do not now exist, we must draw tentative conclusions from many scattered data.

Perhaps the most significant datum is the deeply engraved desire for immortality that manifests itself in the many rituals and beliefs that aim at preserving the human body. On the other hand, the modern, specifically American denial of death by the "beautification" of the body speaks equally for the repression of the fear of dying by merely camouflaging death.

There is only one way—taught by the Buddha, by Jesus, by the Stoics, by Master Eckhart—to truly overcome the fear of dying, and that way is by *not hanging onto life, not experiencing life as a possession*. The fear of dying is not truly what it seems to be: the fear of stopping living. Death does not concern us, Epicurus said, "since while we are, death is not yet here; but when death is here we are no more" (Diogenes Laertius). To be sure, there can be fear of suffering and pain that may precede dying, but this fear is different from that of dying. While the fear of dying may thus seem irrational, this is not so if life is experienced as possession. The fear, then, is not of dying, but of *losing what I have*: the fear of losing my body, my ego, my possessions, and my identity; the fear of facing the abyss of nonidentity, of "being lost."

To the extent that we live in the having mode, we must fear dying. No rational explanation will take away this fear. But it may be diminished, even at the hour of death, by our reassertion of our bond to life, by a response to the love of others that may kindle our own love. Losing our fear of dying should not begin as a preparation for death, but as the continuous effort to *reduce the mode of having and to increase the mode of being*. As Spinoza says, the wise think about life, not about death.

The instruction on how to die is indeed the same as the instruction on how to live. The more we rid ourselves of the craving for possession in all its forms, particularly our ego-boundness, the less strong is the fear of dying, since there is nothing to lose.*

Here, Now—Past, Future

The mode of being exists only in the here and now (*hic et nunc*). The mode of having exists only in time: past, present, and future.

In the having mode we are bound to what we have amassed in the *past*: money, land, fame, social status, knowledge, children, memories. We think about the past, and we feel by *remembering* feelings (or what appear to be feelings) of the past. (This is the essence of sentimentality.) We *are* the past; we can say: "I am what I was."

The *future* is the anticipation of what will become the past. It is experienced in the mode of having as is the past and is expressed when one says: "This person *has* a future," indicating that the individual will *have* many things even though he or she does not now have them. The Ford company's advertising slogan, "There's a Ford in your future," stressed *having* in the future, just as in certain business transactions one buys or sells "commodity futures." The fundamental experience of having is the same, whether we deal with past or future.

The *present* is the point where past and future join, a frontier station in time, but not different in quality from the two realms it connects.

*I restrict this discussion to the fear of dying as such and shall not enter into discussion of an insoluble problem, the pain of suffering that our death can inflict upon those who love us.

Being is not necessarily outside of time, but time is not the dimension that governs being. The painter has to wrestle with color, canvas, and brushes, the sculptor with stone and chisel. Yet the creative act, their "vision" of what they are going to create, transcends time. It occurs in a flash, or in many flashes, but time is not experienced in the vision. The same holds true for the thinkers. Writing down their ideas occurs in time, but conceiving them is a creative event outside of time. It is the same for every manifestation of being. The experience of loving, of joy, of grasping truth does not occur in time, but in the here and now. The *here and now is eternity,* i.e., timelessness. But eternity is not, as popularly misunderstood, indefinitely prolonged time.

One important qualification must be made, though, regarding relationship to the past. Our references here have been to remembering the past, thinking, ruminating about it; in this mode of "having" the past, the past is dead. But one can also bring the past to life. One can experience a situation of the past with the same freshness as if it occurred in the here and now; that is, one can re-create the past, bring it to life (resurrect the dead, symbolically speaking). To the extent that one does so, the past ceases to be the past; it *is* the here and now.

One can also experience the future as if it were the here and now. This occurs when a future state is so fully anticipated in one's own experience that it is only the future "objectively," i.e., in external fact, but not in the subjective experience. This is the nature of genuine utopian thinking (in contrast to utopian daydreaming); it is the basis of genuine faith, which does not need the external realization "in the future" in order to make the experience of it real.

The whole concept of past, present, and future, i.e., of time, enters into our lives due to our bodily existence: the limited duration of our life, the constant demand of our body to be taken care of, the nature of the physical world that we have to use in order to sustain ourselves. Indeed, we cannot live in eternity; being mortal, we cannot ignore or escape time. The rhythm of night and day, of sleep and wakefulness, of growing and aging, the need to sustain ourselves by work and to defend ourselves, all these factors force us to *respect* time if we want to live, and our bodies make us want to live. But that we *respect* time is one thing; that we *submit* to it is another. In the mode of being, we respect time, but we do not submit to it. But this respect for time *becomes submission* when the having mode predominates. In this mode not only things are things, but all that is alive becomes a thing. In the mode of having, time becomes our ruler. In the being mode, time is dethroned; it is no longer the idol that rules our life.

In industrial society time rules supreme. The current mode of production demands that every action be exactly "timed," that not only the endless assembly line conveyor belt but, in a less crude sense, most of our activities be ruled by time. In addition, time not only is time, "time is money." The machine must be used maximally; therefore the machine forces its own rhythm upon the worker.

Via the machine, time has become our ruler. Only in our free hours do we seem to have a certain choice. Yet we usually organize our leisure as we organize our work. Or we rebel against tyrant time by being absolutely lazy. By not doing anything except disobeying time's demands, we have the illusion that we are free, when we are, in fact, only paroled from our time-prison.

PART THREE

THE NEW MAN AND THE NEW SOCIETY

VII

RELIGION, CHARACTER, AND SOCIETY

This chapter deals with the thesis that social change interacts with a change in the social character; that "religious" impulses contribute the energy necessary to move men and women to accomplish drastic social change, and hence, that a new society can be brought about only if a profound change occurs in the human heart—if a new object of devotion takes the place of the present one.*

The Foundations of Social Character

The starting point for these reflections is the statement that the character structure of the average individual and the socioeconomic structure of the society of which he or she is a part are interdependent. I call the blending of the individual psychical sphere and the socioeconomic structure *social character*. (Much earlier, 1932, I had used "libidinous structure of society" to express this phenomenon.) The socioeconomic structure of a society molds the social character of its members so that they *wish* to do

---

*This chapter rests heavily upon my previous work, particularly *Escape from Freedom* (1941) and *Psychoanalysis and Religion* (1950), in both of which are quoted the most important books in the rich literature on this subject.

what they *have* to do. Simultaneously, the social character influences the socioeconomic structure of society, acting either as cement to give further stability to the social
structure or, under special circumstances, as dynamite
that tends to break up the social structure.

Social Character vis-a-vis Social Structure

The relation between social character and social structure is never static, since both elements in this relationship are never-ending processes. A change in either factor
means a change in both. Many political revolutionaries
believe that one must first change the political and economic structure radically, and that then, as a second and
almost necessary step, the human mind will also change:
that the new society, once established, will quasiautomati-
cally produce the new human being. They do not see that
the new elite, being motivated by the same character as
the old one, will tend to recreate the conditions of the old
society in the new sociopolitical institutions the revolution
has created; that the victory of the revolution will be its
defeat as a revolution—although not as a historical phase
that paved the way for the socioeconomic development
that was hobbled in its full development. The French and
Russian revolutions are textbook examples. It is noteworthy that Lenin, who had not believed that quality of
character was important for a person's revolutionary
function, changed his view drastically in the last year of
his life when he sharply saw Stalin's defects of character
and demanded, in his last will, that because of these
defects Stalin should not become his successor.

On the other side are those who claim that first the
nature of human beings must change—their consciousness, their values, their character—and that only then can
a truly human society be built. The history of the human
race proves them wrong. Purely psychical change has
always remained in the private sphere and been restricted
to small oases, or has been completely ineffective when
the preaching of spiritual values was combined with the
practice of the opposite values.

Social Character and "Religious" Needs

The social character has a further and significant function beyond that of serving the needs of society for a certain type of character and satisfying the individual's character-conditioned needs. Social character must fulfill any human being's inherent religious needs. To clarify, "religion" as I use it here does not refer to a system that has necessarily to do with a concept of God or with idols or even to a system perceived as religion, but to *any group-shared system of thought and action that offers the individual a frame of orientation and an object of devotion*. Indeed, in this broad sense of the word no culture of the past or present, and it seems no culture in the future, can be considered as not having religion.

This definition of "religion" does not tell us anything about its specific content. People may worship animals, trees, idols of gold or stone, an invisible god, a saintly person, or a diabolic leader; they may worship their ancestors, their nation, their class or party, money or success. Their religion may be conducive to the development of destructiveness or of love, of domination or of solidarity; it may further their power of reason or paralyze it. They may be aware of their system as being a religious one, different from those of the secular realm, or they may think that they have no religion, and interpret their devotion to certain allegedly secular aims, such as power, money, or success, as nothing but their concern for the practical and the expedient. The question is not one of *religion or not?* but of *which kind of religion?*— whether it is one that furthers human development, the unfolding of specifically human powers, or one that paralyzes human growth.

A specific religion, provided it is effective in motivating conduct, is not a sum total of doctrines and beliefs; it is rooted in a specific character structure of the individual and, inasmuch as it is the religion of a group, in the social character. Thus, our religious attitude may be considered an aspect of our character structure, for *we are what we are devoted to, and what we are devoted to is what motivates our conduct.* Often, however, individuals are not even aware of the real objects of their personal devotion and mistake their "official" beliefs for their real, though *secret* religion. If, for instance, a man worships power while professing a religion of love, the religion of power is his secret religion, while his so-called official religion, for example Christianity, is only an ideology.

The religious need is rooted in the basic conditions of existence of the human *species*. Ours is a species by itself, just as is the species chimpanzee or horse or swallow. Each species can be and is defined by its specific physiological and anatomical characteristics. There is general agreement on the human species in biological terms. I have proposed that the human species—i.e., human nature—can also be defined *psychically*. In the biological evolution of the animal kingdom the human species emerges when two trends in the animal evolution meet. One trend is *the ever-decreasing determination of behavior by instincts* ("instincts" is used here not in the dated sense of instinct as excluding learning but in the sense of organic drives). Even taking into account the many controversial views about the nature of instincts, it is generally accepted that the higher an animal has risen in the stages of evolution, the less is its behavior determined by phylogenetically programmed instincts.

The process of ever-decreasing determination of behavior by instincts can be plotted as a continuum, at the zero end of which we will find the lowest forms of animal evolution with the highest degree of instinctive determination; this decreases along with animal evolution and reaches a certain level with the mammals; it decreases further in the development going up to the primates, and even here we find a great gulf between monkeys and apes (as R. M. Yerkes and A. V. Yerkes have shown in their classic investigation, 1929). In the species *Homo*, instinctive determination has reached its minimum.

The other trend to be found in animal evolution is *the growth of the brain, particularly of the neocortex*. Here, too, we can plot the evolution as a continuum: at one end, the lowest animals, with the most primitive nervous structure and a relatively small number of neurons; at the other, *Homo sapiens,* with a larger and more complex brain structure, especially a neocortex three times the size of that of our primate ancestors, and a truly fantastic number of interneuronal connections.

Considering these data, the human species can be defined as the primate who emerged at the point of evolution where instinctive determination had reached a minimum and the development of the brain a maximum. This combination of minimal instinctive determination and maximal brain development had never occurred before in animal evolution and constitutes, biologically speaking, a completely new phenomenon.

Lacking the capacity to act by the command of instincts while possessing the capacity for self-awareness, reason, and imagination—new qualities that go beyond the capacity for instrumental thinking of even the cleverest primates—the human species needed a *frame of orientation* and an *object of devotion* in order to survive.

Without a map of our natural and social world—a picture of the world and of one's place in it that is structured and has inner cohesion—human beings would be confused and unable to act purposefully and consistently, for there would be no way of orienting oneself, of finding a fixed point that permits one to organize all the impressions that impinge upon each individual. Our world makes sense to us, and we feel certain about our ideas, through the consensus with those around us. Even if the map is wrong, it fulfills its psychological function. But the map has never been entirely wrong—nor has it ever been entirely right. It has always been enough of an approximation to the explanation of phenomena to serve the purpose of living. Only to the degree that the *practice* of life is freed from its contradictions and its irrationality can the map correspond to reality.

The impressive fact is that no culture has been found in which such a frame of orientation does not exist. Neither has any individual. Often individuals may disclaim having any such overall picture and believe that they respond to the various phenomena and incidents of life from case to case, as their judgment guides them. But it can be easily demonstrated that they simply take their own philosophy for granted because to them it is only common sense, and they are unaware that all their concepts rest upon a commonly accepted frame of reference. When such persons are confronted with a fundamentally different total view of life, they judge it as "crazy" or "irrational" or "childish," while they consider themselves as being only "logical." The deep need for a frame of reference is particularly evident in children. At a certain age, children will often make up their own frame of orientation in an ingenious way, using the few data available to them.

But a map is not enough as a guide for action; we also need a goal that tells us where to go. Animals have no such problems. Their instincts provide them with a map as well as with goals. But lacking instinctive determination and having a brain that permits us to think of many directions in which we can go, we need an object of total devotion, a focal point for all our strivings and the basis for all our effective—not only our proclaimed—values. We need such an object of devotion in order to integrate our energies in one direction, to transcend our isolated existence, with all its doubts and insecurities, and to answer our need for a meaning to life.

Socioeconomic structure, character structure, and religious structure are inseparable from each other. If the religious system does not correspond to the prevalent social character, if it conflicts with the social practice of life, it is only an ideology. We have to look behind it for the *real* religious structure, even though we may not be conscious of it as such—unless the human energies inherent in the religious structure of character act as dynamite and tend to undermine the given socioeconomic conditions. However, as there are always individual exceptions to the dominant social character, there are also individual exceptions to the dominant religious character. They are often the leaders of religious revolutions and the founders of new religions.

The "religious" orientation, as the experiential core of all "high" religions, has been mostly perverted in the development of these religions. The way individuals consciously conceive of their personal orientation does not matter; they may be "religious" without considering themselves to be so—or they may be nonreligious, although considering themselves Christian. We have no word to denote the *experiential* content of religion, aside from its conceptual and institutional aspect. Hence, I use quotation marks to denote "religious" in the *experiential*, subjective orientation, regardless of the conceptual structure in which the person's "religiosity" is expressed.*

Is the Western World Christian?

According to the history books and the opinion of most people, Europe's conversion to Christianity took place first within the Roman Empire under Constantine, followed by the conversion of the heathen in Northern Europe by Bonifacius, the "Apostle of the Germans," and others in the eighth century. *But was Europe ever truly Christianized?*

In spite of the affirmative answer generally given to this question, a closer analysis shows that Europe's conversion to Christianity was largely a sham; that at most one could speak of a limited conversion to Christianity from the twelfth to the sixteenth centuries and that for the centuries before and after this period the conversion was, for the most part, one to an ideology and a more or less serious submission to the church; it did not mean a change of heart, i.e., of the character structure, except for numerous genuinely Christian movements.

In these four hundred years Europe had begun to be Christianized. The church tried to enforce the application of Christian principles on the handling of property, prices, and support of the poor. Many partly heretic leaders and sects arose, largely under the influence of mysticism that demanded the return to the principles of Christ, including the condemnation of property. Mysticism, culminating in Master Eckhart, played a decisive role in this antiauthori-

---

*Nobody has dealt with the theme of atheistic religious experience more profoundly and more boldly than has Ernst Bloch (1972).

tarian humanistic movement and, not accidentally, women became prominent as mystical teachers and as students. Ideas of a world religion or of a simple undogmatic Christianity were voiced by many Christian thinkers; even the idea of the God of the Bible became questionable. The theological and nontheological humanists of the Renaissance, in their philosophy and in their Utopias, continued the line of the thirteenth century, and indeed, between the Late Middle Ages (the "Medieval Renaissance") and the Renaissance proper no sharp dividing lines exists. To show the spirit of the High and the Late Renaissance, I quote Frederick B. Artz's summary picture:

> In society, the great mediaeval thinkers held that all men are equal in the sight of God and that even the humblest has an infinite worth. In economics, they taught that work is a source of dignity not of degradation, that no man should be used for an end independent of his welfare, and that justice should determine wages and prices. In politics, they taught that the function of the state is moral, that law and its administration should be imbued with Christian ideas of justice, and that the relations of ruler and ruled should always be founded on reciprocal obligation. The state, property, and the family are all trusts from God to those who control them, and they must be used to further divine purposes. Finally, the mediaeval ideal included the strong belief that all nations and peoples are part of one great community. As Goethe said, "Above the nations is humanity," or as Edith Cavell wrote in 1915 in the margin of her *Imitation of Christ* the night before she was executed, "Patriotism is not enough."

Indeed, had European history continued in the spirit of the thirteenth century, had it developed the spirit of scientific knowledge and individualism slowly and in an evolutionary way, we might now have been in a fortunate position. But reason began to deteriorate into manipulative intelligence and individualism into selfishness. The

short period of Christianization ended and Europe returned to its original paganism.

However the concepts may differ, one belief defines
any branch of Christianity: the belief in Jesus Christ as
the Savior who gave his life out of love for his fellow
creatures. He was the hero of love, a hero without power,
who did not use force, who did not want to rule, who did
not want to *have* anything. He was a hero of being, of
giving, of sharing. These qualities deeply appealed to the
Roman poor as well as to some of the rich, who choked
on their selfishness. Jesus appealed to the hearts of the
people, even though from an intellectual standpoint he
was at best considered to be naïve. This belief in the hero
of love won hundreds of thousands of adherents, many of
whom changed their practice of life, or became martyrs
themselves.

The Christian hero was the martyr, for as in the Jewish
tradition, the highest achievement was to give one's life
for God or for one's fellow beings. The martyr is the
exact opposite of the pagan hero personified in the Greek
and Germanic heroes. The heroes' aim was to conquer, to
be victorious, to destroy, to rob; their fulfillment of life
was pride, power, fame, and superior skill in killing (St.
Augustine compared Roman history with that of a band
of robbers). For the pagan hero a man's worth lay in his
prowess in attaining and holding onto power, and he
gladly died on the battlefield in the moment of victory.
Homer's *Iliad* is the poetically magnificent description of
glorified conquerors and robbers. The martyr's characteristics are *being,* giving, sharing; the hero's, *having,* exploiting, forcing. (It should be added that the formation
of the pagan hero is connected with the patriarchal victory over mother-centered society. Men's dominance of
women is the first act of conquest and the first exploitative
use of force; in all patriarchal societies after the men's
victory, these principles have become the basis of men's
character.)

Which of the two irreconcilably opposed models for
our own development still prevails in Europe? If we look
into ourselves, into the behavior of almost all people, into
our political leaders, it is undeniable that our model of

what is good and valuable is the pagan hero. European–
North American history, in spite of the conversion to the
church, is a history of conquest, pride, greed; our highest
values are: to be stronger than others, to be victorious, to
conquer others and exploit them. These values coincide
with our ideal of "manliness": only the one who can fight
and conquer is a man; anyone who is not strong in the
use of force is weak, i.e., "unmanly."

It is not necessary to prove that the history of Europe
is a history of conquest, exploitation, force, subjugation.
Hardly any period is not characterized by these factors,
no race or class exempted, often including genocide, as
with the American Indians, and even such religious enterprises as the Crusades are no exception. Was this behavior only outwardly economically or politically motivated,
and were the slave traders, the rulers of India, the killers
of Indians, the British who forced the Chinese to open
their land to the import of opium, the instigators of two
World Wars and those who prepare the next war, were all
these Christians in their hearts? Or were perhaps only the
leaders rapacious pagans while the great mass of the
population remained Christians? If this were so, we might
feel more cheerful. Unfortunately, it is not so. To be sure,
the leaders were often more rapacious than their followers because they had more to gain, but they could not
have realized their plans were it not that the wish to
conquer and to be victorious was and still is part of the
social character.

One has only to recall the wild, crazy enthusiasm with
which people participated in the various wars of the past
two centuries—the readiness of millions to risk national
suicide in order to protect the image of "the strongest
power," or of "honor," or of profits. And for another
example, consider the frenzied nationalism of people
watching the contemporary Olympic Games, which allegedly serve the cause of peace. Indeed, the popularity of
the Olympic Games is in itself a symbolic expression of
Western paganism. They celebrate the pagan hero: the
winner, the strongest, the most self-assertive, while over-
looking the dirty mixture of business and publicity that
characterizes the contemporary imitation of the Greek

Olympic Games. In a Christian culture the Passion Play would take the place of Olympic Games; yet the one famous Passion Play we have is the tourist sensation in Oberammergau.

If all this is correct, why do not Europeans and Americans frankly abandon Christianity as not fitting our times? There are several reasons: for example, religious ideology is needed in order to keep people from losing discipline and thus threatening social coherence. But there is a still more important reason: people who are firm believers in Christ as the great lover, the self-sacrificing God, can turn this belief, in an alienated way, into the experience that it is Jesus who loves *for them*. Jesus thus becomes an idol; the belief in him becomes the substitute for one's own act of loving. In a simple, unconscious formula: "Christ does all the loving for us; we can go on in the pattern of the Greek hero, yet we are saved because the alienated 'faith' in Christ is a substitute for the *imitation* of Christ." That Christian belief is also a cheap cover for one's own rapacious attitude goes without saying. Finally, I believe that human beings are so deeply endowed with a need to love that acting as wolves causes us necessarily to have a guilty conscience. Our professed belief in love anesthetizes us to some degree against the pain of the unconscious feeling of guilt for being entirely without love.

"Industrial Religion"

The religious and philosophical development after the end of the Middle Ages is too complex to be treated within the present volume. It can be characterized by the struggle between two principles: the Christian, spiritual tradition in theological or philosophical forms and the pagan tradition of idolatry and inhumanity that assumed many forms in the development of what might be called the "religion of industrialism and the cybernetic era."

Following the tradition of the Late Middle Ages, the humanism of the Renaissance was the first great flowering of the "religious" spirit after the end of the Middle Ages. The ideas of human dignity, of the unity of the human race, of universal political and religious unity found in it

an unencumbered expression. The seventeenth- and eighteenth-century Enlightenment expressed another great
flowering of humanism. Carl Becker (1932) has shown to
what extent the Enlightenment philosophy expressed the
"religious attitude" that we find in the theologians of the
thirteenth century: "If we examine the foundation of this
faith, we find that at every turn the *Philosophers* betrayed
their debt to medieval thought without being aware of it."
The French Revolution, to which Enlightenment philosophy had given birth, was more than a political revolution. As Tocqueville noted (quoted by Becker), it was a
"political revolution which functioned in the manner and
which took on in some sense the aspect of a *religious
revolution* [emphasis added]. Like Islamism and the
Protestant revolt it overflowed the frontiers of countries
and nations and was extended by preaching and propaganda."

Radical humanism in the nineteenth and twentieth centuries is described later on, in my discussion of the
humanist protest against the paganism of the industrial
age. But to provide a base for that discussion we must
now look at the new paganism that has developed side by
side with humanism, threatening at the present moment of
history to destroy us.

The change that prepared the first basis for the development of the "industrial religion" was the elimination,
by Luther, of the motherly element in the church. Although it may appear an unnecessary detour, I must dwell
on this problem for a while, because it is important to our
understanding of the development of the new religion and
the new social character.

Societies have been organized according to two principles: patricentric (or patriarchal) and matricentric (or
matriarchal). The matricentric principle, as J. J. Bachofen and L. H. Morgan have shown for the first time, is
centered in the figure of the loving mother. The motherly
principle is that of *unconditional love;* the mother loves
her children not because they please her, but because they
are her (or another woman's) children. For this reason
the mother's love cannot be acquired by good behavior,
nor can it be lost by sinning. Motherly love is *mercy* and

compassion (in Hebrew *rachamim,* the root of which is *rechem,* the "womb").

Fatherly love, on the contrary, is *conditional;* it depends on the achievements and good behavior of the child; father loves that child most who is most like him, i.e., whom he wishes to inherit his property. Father's love can be lost, but it can also be regained by repentance and renewed submission. Father's love is *justice.*

The two principles, the feminine-motherly and the masculine-fatherly, correspond not only to the presence of a masculine and feminine side in any human being but specifically to the need for mercy *and* justice in every man and woman. The deepest yearning of human beings seems to be a constellation in which the two poles (motherliness and fatherliness, female and male, mercy and justice, feeling and thought, nature and intellect) are united in a synthesis, in which both sides of the polarity lose their mutual antagonism and, instead, color each other. While such a synthesis cannot be fully reached in a patriarchal society, it existed to some extent in the Roman Church. The Virgin, the church as the all-loving mother, the pope and the priest as motherly figures represented motherly, unconditional, all-forgiving love, side by side with the fatherly elements of a strict, patriarchal bureaucracy with the pope at the top ruling by power.

Corresponding to these motherly elements in the religious system was the relationship toward nature in the process of production: the work of the peasant as well as of the artisan was not a hostile exploitative attack against nature. It was cooperation with nature: not raping but transforming nature according to its own laws.

Luther established a purely patriarchal form of Christianity in Northern Europe that was based on the urban middle class and the secular princes. The essence of this new social character is submission under patriarchal authority, with *work* as the only way to obtain love and approval.

Behind the Christian façade arose a new *secret* religion, "industrial religion," that is rooted in the character structure of modern society, but is not recognized as "religion." The industrial religion is incompatible with genuine

Christianity. It reduces people to servants of the economy and of the machinery that their own hands build.

The industrial religion had its basis in a new social character. Its center was fear of and submission to powerful male authorities, cultivation of the sense of guilt for disobedience, dissolution of the bonds of human solidarity by the supremacy of self-interest and mutual antagonism. The "sacred" in industrial religion was work, property, profit, power, even though it furthered individualism and freedom within the limits of its general principles. By transforming Christianity into a strictly patriarchal religion it was still possible to express the industrial religion in Christian terminology.

The "Marketing Character" and "Cybernetic Religion"

The most important fact for understanding both the character and the secret religion of contemporary human society is the change in the social character from the earlier era of capitalism to the second part of the twentieth century. The authoritarian-obsessive-hoarding character that had begun to develop in the sixteenth century, and continued to be the dominant character structure at least in the middle classes until the end of the nineteenth century, was slowly blended with or replaced by the *marketing characyer*. (I described the blends of various character orientations in *Man for Himself*.)

I have called this phenomenon the marketing character because it is based on experiencing oneself as a commodity, and one's value not as "use value" but as "exchange value." The living being becomes a commodity on the "personality market." The principle of evaluation is the same on both the personality and the commodity markets: on the one, personalities are offered for sale; on the other, commodities. Value in both cases is their exchange value, for which "use value" is a necessary but not a sufficient condition.

Although the proportion of skill and human qualities on the one hand and personality on the other hand as prerequisites for success varies, the "personality factor" always plays a decisive role. Success depends largely on how well persons sell themselves on the market, how well they get their "personality" across, how nice a "package" they are; whether they are "cheerful," "sound," "aggressive," "reliable," "ambitious"; furthermore, what their family backgrounds are, what clubs they belong to, and whether they know the "right" people. The type of personality required depends to some degree on the special field in which a person may choose to work. A stockbroker, a salesperson, a secretary, a railroad executive, a college professor, or a hotel manager must each offer a different kind of personality that, regardless of their differences, must fulfill one condition: to be in demand.

What shapes one's attitude toward oneself is the fact that skill and equipment for performing a given task are not sufficient; one must be able to win in competition with many others in order to have success. If it were enough for the purpose of making a living to rely on what one knows and what one can do, one's self-esteem would be in proportion to one's capacities, that is, to one's use value. But since success depends largely on how one sells one's personality, one experiences oneself as a commodity or, rather, simultaneously as the seller *and* the commodity to be sold. A person is not concerned with his or her life and happiness, but with becoming salable.

The aim of the marketing character is complete adaptation, so as to be desirable under all conditions of the personality market. The marketing character personalities do not even *have* egos (as people in the nineteenth century did) to hold onto, that belong to them, that do not change. For they constantly change their egos, according to the principle: "I am as you desire me."

Those with the marketing character structure are without goals, except moving, doing things with the greatest efficiency; if asked *why* they must move so fast, why things have to be done with the greatest efficiency, they have no genuine answer, but offer rationalizations, such as, "in order to create more jobs," or "in order to keep the company growing." They have little interest (at least consciously) in philosophical or religious questions, such as *why* one lives, and *why* one is going in this direction rather than in another. They have their big, ever-changing egos, but none has a self, a core, a sense of identity. The "identity crisis" of modern society is actually the crisis produced by the fact that its memebers have become selfless instruments, whose identity rests upon their participation in the corporations (or other giant bureaucracies). Where there is no authentic self, there can be no identity.

The marketing character neither loves nor hates. These "old-fashioned" emotions do not fit into a character structure that functions almost entirely on the cerebral level and avoids feelings, whether good or evil ones, because they interfere with the marketing characters' main purpose: selling and exchanging—or to put it even more precisely, *functioning* according to the logic of the "megamachine" of which they are a part, without asking any questions except how well they function, as indicated by their advancement in the bureaucracy.

Since the marketing characters have no deep attachment to themselves or to others, they do not care, in any deep sense of the word, not because they are so selfish but because their relations to others and to themselves are so thin. This may also explain why they are not concerned with the dangers of nuclear and ecological catastrophes, even though they know all the data that point to these dangers. That they are not concerned with the danger to their personal lives might still be explained by the assumption that they have great courage and unselfishness; but the lack of concern even for their children and grandchildren excludes such explanation. The lack of concern on all these levels is the result of the loss of any emotional ties, even to those "nearest" to them. The fact is, nobody is close to the marketing characters; neither are they close to themselves.

The puzzling question why contemporary human beings love to buy and to consume, and yet are so little attached to what they buy, finds its most significant answer in the marketing character phenomenon. The marketing characters' lack of attachment also makes them indifferent to things. What matters is perhaps the prestige or the comfort that things give, but things per se have no substance. They are utterly expendable, along with friends or lovers, who are expendable, too, since no deeper tie exists to any of them.

The marketing character goal, *"proper functioning"* under the given circumstances, makes them respond to the world mainly cerebrally. Reason in the sense of *understanding* is an exclusive quality of *Homo sapiens; manipulative intelligence* as a tool for the achievement of practical purposes is common to animals and humans. Manipulative intelligence without reason is dangerous because it makes people move in directions that may be self-destructive from the standpoint of reason. In fact, the more brilliant the uncontrolled manipulative intelligence is, the more dangerous it is.

It was no less a scientist than Charles Darwin who demonstrated the consequences and the human tragedy of a purely scientific, alienated intellect. He writes in his autobiography that until his thirtieth year he had intensely enjoyed music and poetry and pictures, but that for many years afterward he lost all his taste for these interests: "My mind seems to have become a kind of machine for grinding general laws out of large collections of fact. . . . The loss of these tastes is a loss of happiness, and may possibly be injurious to the intellect, and more probably to the moral character, by enfeebling the emotional part of our nature." (Quoted by E. P. Schumacher; q.v.)

The process Darwin describes here has continued since his time at a rapid pace; the separation from reason and heart is almost complete. It is of special interest that this deterioration of reason had not taken place in the majority of the leading investigators in the most exacting and revolutionary sciences (in theoretical physics, for example) and that they were people who were deeply concerned with philosophical and spiritual questions. I refer to such individuals as A. Einstein, N. Bohr, L. Szillard, W. Heisenberg, E. Schrödinger.

The supremacy of cerebral, manipulative thinking goes together with an atrophy of emotional life. Since it is not cultivated or needed, but rather an impediment to optimal functioning, emotional life has remained stunted and never matured beyond the level of a child's. As a result the marketing characters are peculiarly naive as far as emotional problems are concerned. They may be attracted by "emotional people," but because of their own naiveté, they often cannot judge whether such people are genuine or fakers. This may explain why so many fakers can be successful in the spiritual and religious fields; it may also explain why politicians who portray strong emotions have a strong appeal for the marketing character—and why the marketing character cannot discriminate between a genuinely religious person and the public relations product who fakes strong religious emotions.

The term "marketing character" is by no means the only one to describe this type. It can also be described by using a Marxian term, the *alienated character;* persons of this character are alienated from their work, from themselves, from other human beings, and from nature. In psychiatric terms the marketing person could be called a schizoid character; but the term may be slightly misleading, because a schizoid person living with other schizoid persons and performing well and being successful, lacks the feeling of uneasiness that the schizoid character has in a more "normal" environment.

During the final revision of the manuscript of this book I had the opportunity to read Michael Maccoby's forthcoming work *The Gamesmen: The New Corporate Leaders* in manuscript. In this penetrating study Maccoby analyzes the character structure of two hundred and fifty executives, managers, and engineers in two of the best-run large companies in the United States. Many of his findings confirm what I have described as features of the cybernetic person, particularly the predominance of the cerebral along with the underdevelopment of the emotional sphere. Considering that the executives and managers described by Maccoby are or will be among the leaders of American society, the social importance of Maccoby's findings is substantial.

The following data, drawn by Maccoby from his three to twenty personal interviews with each member of the group studied, give us a clear picture of this character type.*

Deep scientific interest in understanding, dynamic sense of the work, animated	0%
Centered, enlivening, craftsmanlike, but lacks deeper scientific interest in the nature of things	22%
The work itself stimulates interest, which is not self-sustained	58%
Moderate productive, not centered. Interest in work is essentially instrumental, to ensure security, income	18%
Passive unproductive, diffused	2%
Rejecting of work, rejects the real world	0%
	100%

Two features are striking: (1) deep interest in understanding ("reason") is absent, and (2) for the vast majority either the stimulation of their work is not self-sustaining or the work is essentially a means for ensuring economic security.

In complete contrast is the picture of what Maccoby calls "the love scale":

Loving, affirmative, creatively stimulating	0%
Responsible, warm, affectionate, but not deeply loving	5%
Moderate interest in another person, with more loving possibilities	40%
Conventional concern, decent, role oriented	41%
Passive, unloving, uninterested	13%
Rejecting of life, hardened heart	1%
	100%

No one in the study could be characterized as deeply loving, although 5 percent show up as being "warm and affectionate." All the rest are listed as having moderate interest, or conventional concern, or as unloving, or outright rejecting of life—indeed a striking picture of emo-

---

*Reprinted by permission. Cf. a parallel study by Ignacio Millan, *The Character of Mexican Executives*, to be published soon.

tional underdevelopment in contrast to the prominence of cerebralism.

The "cybernetic religion" of the marketing character corresponds to that total character structure. Hidden behind the façade of agnosticism or Christianity is a thoroughly pagan religion, although people are not conscious of it as such. This pagan religion is difficult to describe, since it can only be inferred from what people do (and do *not* do) and not from their conscious thoughts about religion or dogmas of a religious organization. Most striking, at first glance, is that Man has made himself into a god because he has acquired the technical capacity for a "second creation" of the world, replacing the first creation by the God of traditional religion. We can also formulate: We have made the machine into a god and have become godlike by serving the machine. It matters little the formulation we choose; what matters is that human beings, in the state of their greatest real *impotence, imagine* themselves in connection with science and technique to be *omnipotent.*

The more we are caught in our isolation, in our lack of emotional response to the world, and at the same time the more unavoidable a catastrophic end seems to be, the more malignant becomes the new religion. We cease to be the masters of technique and become instead its slaves— and technique, once a vital element of creation, shows its other face as the goddess of destruction (like the Indian goddess Kali), to which men and women are willing to sacrifice themselves and their children. While consciously still hanging onto the hope for a better future, cybernetic humanity represses the fact that they have become worshipers of the goddess of destruction.

This thesis has many kinds of proof, but none more compelling than these two: that the great (and even some smaller) powers continue to build nuclear weapons of ever-increasing capacity for destruction and do not arrive at the one sane solution—destruction of all nuclear weapons and the atomic energy plants that deliver the material for nuclear weapons—and that virtually nothing is done to end the danger of ecological catastrophe. In short, nothing serious is being done to plan for the survival of the human race.

The Humanist Protest

The dehumanization of the social character and the rise of the industrial and cybernetic religions led to a protest movement, to the emergence of a new humanism, that has its roots in Christian and philosopical humanism from the Late Middle Ages to the Age of Enlightenment. This protest found expression in theistic Christian as well as in pantheistic or nontheistic philosophical formulations. It came from two opposite sides: from the romantics, who were politically conservatives, and from the Marxian and other socialists (and some anarchists). The right and the left were unanimous in their critique of the industrial system and the damage it did to human beings. Catholic thinkers, such as Franz von Baader, and conservative political leaders, such as Benjamin Disraeli, formulated the problem, sometimes in identical ways to those of Marx.

The two sides differed in the ways they thought human beings could be saved from the danger of being transformed into things. The romantics on the right believed that the only way was to stop the unhindered "progress" of the industrial system and to return to previous forms of the social order, though with some modifications.

The protest from the left may be called *radical humanism,* even though it was sometimes expressed in theistic and sometimes in nontheistic terms. The socialists believed that the economic development could not be halted, that one could not return to a previous form of social order, and that the only way to salvation lay in going forward and creating a new society that would free people from alienation, from submission to the machine, from the fate of being dehumanized. Socialism was the synthesis of medieval religious tradition and the post-Renaissance spirit of scientific thinking and political action. It was, like Buddhism, a "religious" mass movement that, even though speaking in secular and atheistic terms,

aimed at the liberation of human beings from selfishness
and greed.

At least a brief commentary is necessary to explain my
characterization of Marxian thought, in view of its complete perversion by Soviet communism and reformist
Western socialism to a materialism aimed at achieving
wealth for everybody. As Hermann Cohen, Ernst Bloch,
and a number of other scholars have stated during the
past decades, socialism was the secular expression of
prophetic Messianism. Perhaps the best way to demonstrate this is to quite from the Code of Maimonides his
characterization of the Messianic Time:

> The Sages and Prophets did not long for the days
> of the Messiah that Israel might exercise dominion
> over the world, or rule over the heathens, or be
> exalted by the nations, or that it might eat and drink
> and rejoice. Their aspiration was that Israel be free
> to devote itself to the Law and its wisdom, with no
> one to oppress or disturb it, and thus be worthy of
> life in the world to come.
>
> In that era there will be neither famine nor war,
> neither jealousy nor strife. Earthly goods* will be
> abundant, comforts within the reach of all. The one
> preoccupation of the whole world will be to know
> the Lord. Hence Israelites will be very wise, they will
> know the things that are now concealed and will
> attain an understanding of their creator to the utmost
> capacity of the human mind, as it is written: For the
> earth shall be full of the knowledge of the Lord, as
> the waters cover the sea (Isaiah 11:9).

In this description the goal of history is to enable
human beings to devote themselves entirely to the study
of wisdom and the knowledge of God; not power or
luxury. The Messianic Time is one of universal peace,
absence of envy, and material abundance. This picture is
very close to the concept of the goal of life as Marx

*My translation from the Hebrew text, instead of "blessings"
in the Hershman translation, published by Yale University Press.

expressed it toward the end of the third volume of his *Capital:*

> The realm of freedom does not commence until the point is passed where labor under the compulsion of necessity and of external utility is required. In the very nature of things it lies beyond the sphere of material production in the strict meaning of the term. Just as the savage must wrestle with nature, in order to satisfy his wants, in order to maintain his life and reproduce it, so civilized man has to do it, and he must do it in all forms of society and under all possible modes of production. With his development the realm of natural necessity expands, because his wants increase; but at the same time the forces of production increase, by which these wants are satisfied. The freedom in this field cannot consist of anything else but of the fact that socialized man, the associated producers, regulate their interchange with nature rationally, bring it under their common control, instead of being ruled by it as by some blind power; that they accomplish their task with the least expenditure of energy and under conditions most adequate to their human nature and *most worthy of it.* But it always remains a realm of necessity. Beyond it begins that *development of human power which is its own end,* the true realm of freedom, which, however, can flourish only upon that realm of necessity as its basis. The shortening of the working day is its fundamental premise. [Emphasis added.]

Marx, like Maimonides—and in contrast to Christian and to other Jewish teachings of salvation—does not postulate a final eschatological solution; the discrepancy between Man and nature remains, but the realm of necessity is brought under human control as much as possible: "But it always remains a realm of necessity." The goal is *"that development of human power which is its own end, the true realm of freedom"* (emphasis added). Maimonides' view that "the preoccupation of the whole world will be to know the Lord" is to Marx the "development of human power . . . [as] its own end."

Having and being as two different forms of human existence are at the center of Marx's ideas for the emergence of new Man. With these modes Marx proceeds from economic to psychological and anthropological categories, which are, as we have seen in our discussion of the Old and New Testaments and Eckhart, at the same time fundamental "religious" categories. Marx wrote: "Private property has made us so stupid and partial that an object is only ours when we have it, when it exists for us as capital or when it is directly eaten, drunk, worn, inhabited, etc., in short, *utilized* in some way.... Thus *all* the physical and intellectual senses have been replaced by the simple alienation of *all* these senses; the sense of *having*. The human being had to be reduced to this absolute poverty in order to be able to give birth to all his inner wealth. (On the category of *having* see Hess in *Einundzwanzig Bogen*.)"*

Marx's concept of being and having is summarized in his sentence: "The less you *are* and the less you express your life—the more you *have* and the greater is your alienated life.... Everything the economist takes away from you in the way of life and humanity, he restores to you in the form of money and wealth."

The "sense of having" about which Marx speaks here is precisely the same as the "egoboundness" of which Eckhart speaks, the craving for things and for one's ego. Marx refers to the *having mode of existence,* not to possession as such, not to unalienated private property as such. The goal is not luxury and wealth, nor is it poverty; in fact, *both* luxury and poverty are looked upon by Marx as vices. The goal is "to give birth."

What is this act of giving birth? It is the active, unalienated expression of our faculty toward the corresponding objects. Marx contiues: "All his [Man's] *human* relations to the world—seeing, hearing, smelling, tasting, touching, thinking, observing, feeling, desiring,

---

*This and the following passages are from Marx's *Economic and Philosophical Manuscripts,* translated in *Marx's Concept of Man.*

acting, loving—in short all the organs of his individuality
... are in their objective action [their *action in relation to
the object*] the appropriation of this object, the appropriation of human reality." This is the form of appropriation in the mode of *being,* not in the mode of having.
Marx expressed this form of nonalienated activity in the
following passage:

> Let us assume *man* to be *man,* and his relation to the
> world to be a human one. Then love can only be
> exchanged for love, trust for trust, etc. If you wish to
> enjoy art, you must be an artistically cultivated person;
> if you wish to influence other people, you must be a
> person who really has a stimulating and encouraging
> effect upon others. Every one of your relations to man
> and to nature must be a *specific expression,* corre-
> sponding to the object of your will, of your *real individ-
> ual* life. If you love without evoking love in return, i.e.,
> if you are not able, by the *manifestation* of yourself as
> a loving person, to make yourself a *beloved person,*
> then your love is impotent and a misfortune.

But Marx's ideas were soon perverted, perhaps because
he lived a hundred years too soon. Both he and Engels
thought that capitalism had already reached the end of its
possibilities and, hence, that the revolution was just
around the corner. But they were thoroughly mistaken, as
Engels was to state after Marx's death. They had pronounced their new teaching at the very height of capitalist
development and did not foresee that it would take more
than a hundred years for capitalism's decline and the final
crisis to begin. It was a historical necessity that an anti-
capitalist idea, propagated at the very peak of capitalism,
had to be utterly transformed into the capitalist spirit if it
was to be successful. And this is what actually happened.

Western social democrats and their bitter opponents,
communists within and without the Soviet Union, transformed socialism into a purely economic concept, the goal
of which was maximum consumption, maximun use of
machines. Khrushchev, with his concept of "goulash"

communism, in his simple and folksy manner let the truth out of the bag: The aim of socialism was to give the whole population the same pleasure of consumption as capitalism gave only to a minority. Socialism and communism were built on the bourgeois concept of materialism. Some phrases of Marx's earlier writings (which, on the whole, were denigrated as "idealistic" errors of the "young" Marx) were recited as ritualistically as the words of the gospels are cited in the West.

That Marx lived at the height of capitalist development had another consequence: as a child of his time Marx could not help adopting attitudes and concepts current in bourgeois thought and practice. Thus, for instance, certain authoritarian inclinations in his personality as well as in his writings were molded by the patriarchal bourgeois spirit rather than by the spirit of socialism. He followed the pattern of the classical economists in his construction of "scientific" versus "utopian" socialism. Just as the economists claimed that economics was following its own laws quite independently of human will, Marx sensed the need to prove that socialism would *necessarily* develop according to the laws of economics. Consequently, he sometimes tended to develop formulations that could be misunderstood as deterministic, not giving a sufficient role to human will and imagination in the historical process. Such unintended concessions to the spirit of capitalism facilitated the process of perverting Marx's system into one that was not fundamentally different from capitalism.

If Marx had pronounced his ideas today, at the beginning—and rapidly increasing—decline of capitalism, his *real* message would have had a chance to be influential or even victorious, provided one can make such a historical conjecture. As it is, even the words "socialism" and "communism" are compromised. At any rate, every socialist or communist party that could claim to represent Marxian thought would have to be based on the conviction that the Soviet regimes are *not* socialist systems in any sense, that socialism is incompatible with a bureaucratic, thing-centered, consumption-oriented social system, that it is incompatible with the materialism and cerebralization that characterize the Soviet, like the capitalist, system.

The corruption of socialism explains the fact that genuine radical humanist thoughts often come from groups and individuals who were not identified with the ideas of Marx or who were even opposed to them, sometimes after having been active members of the communist movement.

While it is impossible to mention here all the radical humanists of the post-Marxian period, some examples of their thinking are given on the following pages. Though the conceptualizations of these radical humanists differed widely, and sometimes seem to contradict each other completely, they all share the following ideas and attitudes:

- that production must serve the real needs of the people, not the demands of the economic system:
- that a new relation must be established between people and nature, one of cooperation not of exploitation;
- that mutual antagonism must be replaced by solidarity;
- that the aim of all social arrangements must be human well-being and the prevention of ill-being;
- that not maximum consumption but sane consumption that furthers well-being must be striven for;
- that the individual must be an active, not a passive, participant in social life.*

Albert Schweitzer starts from the radical premise of the imminent crisis of Western culture. "It is obvious to everybody," he states, "that we are in a process of cultural self-destruction. What is left is also not secure any more. It still stands because it was not exposed to the destructive pressure to which the rest has already succumbed. But it too is built on gravel [Geröll]. The next landslide [Bergrutsch] can take it along. ... The cultural capacity of modern Man is diminished because the cir-

*The socialist humanists' views may be found in E. Fromm, ed., Socialist Humanism.

cumstances which surround him diminish him and damage him psychically."*

Characterizing the industrial being as "unfree ... unconcentrated ... incomplete ... in danger of losing his humanity," he continues:

> Because society with its developed organization exercises a hitherto unknown power over Man, Man's dependency on it has grown to a degree that he almost has ceased to live a mental [*geistig*] existence of his own. ... Thus we have entered a new Middle Ages. By a general act of will freedom of thought has been put out of function, because many give up thinking as free individuals, and are guided by the collective to which they belong. ... With the sacrifice of independence of thought we have—and how could it be otherwise—lost faith in truth. Our intellectual-emotional life is disorganized. *The overorganization of our public affairs culminates in the organization of thoughtlessness* [emphasis added].

He sees industrial society characterized not only by lack of freedom but also by "overeffort" (*Überanstrengung*). "For two or three centuries many individuals have lived only as *working* beings and not as *human* beings." The human substance is stunted and in the upbringing of children by such stunted parents, an essential factor for their human development is lacking. "Later on, himself subjected to overoccupation, the adult person succumbs more and more to the need for superficial distraction. ... *Absolute passivity, diverting attention from and forgetting of oneself are a physical need for him*" (emphasis added). As a consequence Schweitzer pleads for reduction of work and against overconsumption and luxury.

Schweitzer, the Protestant theologian, insists, as does Eckhart, the Dominican monk, that Man's task is not to

---

*This and the following Schweitzer passages are my translations of quotations from *Die Schuld der Philosophie an dem Niedergang der Kultur*, first published in 1923, but sketched from 1900 to 1917.

retire into an atmosphere of spiritual egotism, remote from the affairs of the world, but to lead an active life in which one tries to contribute to the spiritual perfection of society. "If among modern individuals there are so few whose human and ethical sentiments are intact, not the least reason is the fact that they sacrifice constantly their personal morality on the altar of the fatherland, *instead of being in constant living interchange with the collective and of giving it the power which drives the collective to its perfection*" (emphasis added).

He concludes that the present cultural and social structure drives toward a catastrophe, from which only a new Renaissance "much greater than the old one will arise"; that we must renew ourselves in a new belief and attitude, unless we want to perish. "Essential in this Renaissance will be the principle of activity, which rational thinking gives into our hands, the only rational and pragmatic principle of the historical development produced by Man. . . . I have confidence in my faith *that this revolution will occur if we decide to become thinking human beings*" (emphasis added).

It is probably because Schweitzer was a theologian and is best known, at least philosophically, for his concept of "reverence for life" as the basis of ethics that people have generally ignored that he was one of the most radical critics of industrial society, debunking its myth of progress and general happiness. He recognized the decay of human society and the world through the practice of industrialized life; at the beginning of this century he already saw the weakness and dependency of the people, the destructive effect of obsessional work, the need for less work and less consumption. He postulated the necessity for a Renaissance of collective life that would be organized by the spirit of solidarity and reverence for life.

This presentation of Schweitzer's thought should not be concluded without pointing to the fact that Schweitzer, in contrast to the metaphysical optimism of Christianity, was a metaphysical skeptic. This is one of the reasons he was strongly attracted by Buddhist thought, in which life has no meaning that is given and guaranteed by a supreme being. He came to this conclusion: "If one takes the world as it is, it is impossible to endow it with meaning in which the aims and goals of Man and of Mankind make sense." The only meaningful way of life is activity in the world; not activity in general but the activity of giving and caring for fellow creatures. Schweitzer gave this answer in his writing and by living it.

There is a remarkable kinship in the ideas of the Buddha, Eckhart, Marx, and Schweitzer: their radical demand for giving up the having orientation; their insistence on complete independence; their metaphysical skepticism; their godless religiosity,* and their demand for social activity in the spirit of care and human solidarity. However, these teachers are sometimes unconscious of these elements. For instance, Eckhart is usually unconscious of his nontheism; Marx, of his religiosity. The matter of interpretation, especially of Eckhart and Marx, is so complex that it is impossible to give an adequate presentation of the nontheistic religion of caring activism that makes these teachers the founders of a new religiosity fitting the necessities of new Man. In a sequel to this volume I hope to analyze the ideas of these teachers.

Even authors whom one cannot call radical humanists, since they hardly transcend the transpersonal, mechanistic attitude of our age (such as the authors of the two reports commissioned by the Club of Rome), do not fail to see that a radical inner human change is the only alternative to economic catastrophe. Mesarovic and Pestel demand a "new world consciousness ... a new ethic in the use of material resources ... a new attitude toward nature, based on harmony rather than on conquest ... a sense of identification with future generations. ... For the first time in Man's life on earth, he is being asked to refrain from doing what he can do; he is being asked to restrain his economic and technological advancement, or at least to direct it differently from before; he is being asked by all the future generations of the earth to share

*In a letter to E. R. Jacobi, Schweitzer wrote that the "religion of love can exist without a world-ruling personality" (*Divine Light*, 2, No. 1 [1967]).

his good fortune with the unfortunate—not in a spirit of charity but in a spirit of necessity. He is being asked to concentrate now on the organic growth of the total world system. Can he, in good conscience, say no?" They conclude that without these fundamental human changes, "*Homo sapiens* is as good as doomed."

The study has some shortcomings—to me the most outstanding one being that it does not consider the political, social, and psychological factors that stand in the way of any change. To indicate the trend of necessary changes in general is useless until it is followed up by a serious attempt to consider the real obstacles that impede all their suggestions. (It is to be hoped that the Club of Rome comes to grips with the problem of those social and political changes that are the preconditions for attaining the general goals.) Nevertheless the fact remains that these authors have attempted for the first time to show the economic needs and resources of the whole world, and that, as I wrote in the Introduction, for the first time a demand is made for an ethical change, not as a consequence of ethical beliefs but as the rational consequence of economic analysis.

Within the past few years, a considerable number of books in the United States and in Germany have raised the same demand: to subordinate economy to the needs of the people, first for our sheer survival, second for our well-being. (I have read or examined about thirty-five such books, but the number available is at least twice that.) Most of these authors agree that material increase of consumption does not necessarily mean increase in well-being; that a characterological and spiritual change must go together with the necessary social changes; that unless we stop wasting our natural resources and destroying the ecological conditions for human survival, catastrophe within a hundred years is foreseeable. I mention here only a few of the outstanding representatives of this new humanistic economy.

The economist E. F. Schumacher shows in his book *Small Is Beautiful* that our failures are the result of our successes, and that our techniques must be subordinated to our real human needs. "Economy as a content of life is a deadly illness," he writes, "because infinite growth does not fit into a finite world. That economy *should not* be the content of life has been told to mankind by all its great teachers; that it *cannot* be is evident today. If one wants to describe the deadly illness in more detail, one can say that it is similar to an addiction, like alcoholism or drug addiction. It does not matter too much whether this addiction appears in a more egotistical or more altruistic form, whether it seeks its satisfaction only in a crude materialistic way or also in an artistically, culturally, or scientifically refined way. Poison is poison, even if wrapped in silver paper.... If spiritual culture, the culture of the inner Man, is neglected, then selfishness remains the dominating power in Man and a system of selfishness, like capitalism, fits this orientation better than a system of love for one's fellow beings."

Schumacher has translated his principles by devising minimachines that are adapted to the needs of nonindustrialized countries. It is especially noteworthy that his books are more popular every year—and not by a big advertising campaign but by the word-of-mouth propaganda of his readers.

Paul Ehrlich and Anne Ehrlich are two American authors whose thinking is similar to Schumacher's. In their *Population, Resources, Environment: Issues in Human Ecology* they present the following conclusions about "the present world situation":

1. Considering present technology and patterns of behavior our planet is grossly overpopulated now.
2. The large absolute number of people and the rate of population growth are major hindrances to solving human problems.
3. The limits of human capability to produce food by conventional means have very nearly been reached. Problems of supply and distribution already have resulted in roughly half of humanity being undernourished or malnourished. Some 10–20 million people are starving to death annually now.
4. Attempts to increase food production further will tend to accelerate the deterioration of our environ-

ment, which in turn will eventually *reduce* the capacity of the earth to produce food. It is not clear whether environmental decay has now gone so far as to be essentially irreversible; it is possible that the capacity of the planet to support human life has been permanently impaired. Such technological "successes" as automobiles, pesticides, and inorganic nitrogen fertilizers are major causes of environmental deterioration.

5. There is reason to believe that population growth increases the probability of a lethal worldwide plague and of a thermonuclear war. Either could provide an undersirable "death rate solution" to the population problem; each is potentially capable of destroying civilization and even of driving *Homo sapiens* to extinction.

6. There is no technological panacea for the complex of problems composing the population-food-environment crisis, although technology properly applied in such areas as pollution abatement, communications, and fertility control can provide massive assistance. *The basic solutions involve dramatic and rapid changes in human attitudes,* especially those relating to reproductive behavior, economic growth, technology, the environment, and conflict resolution. [Emphasis added.]

E. Eppler's *Ende oder Wende* (End or change) is another recent work that bears mention. Eppler's ideas are similar to Schumacher's, though less radical, and his position is perhaps especially interesting because he is the leader of the Social Democratic party in Baden-Württemberg and a convinced Protestant. Two books I wrote are of the same orientation, *The Sane Society* and *The Revolution of Hope*.

Even among the Soviet bloc writers, where the idea of the restriction of production has always been tabu, voices are beginning to suggest that consideration be given to an economy without growth. W. Harich, a dissident Marxist in the German Democratic Republic, proposes a static, worldwide economic balance, which alone can guarantee equality and avert the danger of irreparable damage to the biosphere. Also, in 1972 some of the most outstanding natural scientists, economists, and geographers in the Soviet Union met to discuss "Man and His Environment." On their agenda were the results of the Club of Rome studies, which they considered in a sympathetic and respectful spirit, pointing to the considerable merits of the studies, even though not agreeing with them. (See "Technologie und Politik" in the Bibliography, for a report of this meeting.)

The most important contemporary anthropological and historical expression of the humanism that is common to these various attempts at humanist social reconstruction is to be found in L. Mumford's *The Pentagon of Power* and in all his previous books.

equality and avert the danger of irreparable damage to

VIII

CONDITIONS FOR HUMAN CHANGE AND THE FEATURES OF THE NEW MAN

Assuming the premise is right—that only a fundamental
change in human character from a preponderance of the
having mode to a predominantly being mode of existence
can save us from a psychologic and economic catastrophe
—the question arises: Is large-scale characterological
change possible, and if so, how can it be brought about?

I suggest that human character *can* change if these
conditions exist:

1. We are suffering and are aware that we are.
2. We recognize the origin of our ill-being.
3. We recognize that there is a way of overcoming our
   ill-being.
4. We accept that in order to overcome our ill-being
   we must follow certain norms for living and change
   our present practice of life.

These four points correspond to the Four Noble Truths
that form the basis of the Buddha's teaching dealing with
the general condition of human existence, though not with
cases of human ill-being due to specific individual or
social circumstances.

The same principle of change that characterizes the methods of the Buddha also underlies Marx's idea of salvation. In order to understand this it is necessary to be aware that for Marx, as he himself said, communism was not a final goal, but a step in the historical development that was to liberate human beings from those socioeconomic and political conditions that make people inhuman —prisoners of things, machines, and their own greed.

Marx's first step was to show the working class of his time, the most alienated and miserable class, *that* they suffered. He tried to destroy the illusions that tended to cover the workers' awareness of their misery. His second step was to show the *causes* of this suffering, which he points out are in the nature of capitalism and the character of greed and avarice and dependence that the capitalistic system produces. This analysis of the cause of the workers' suffering (but not *only* theirs) contributed the main thrust of Marx's work, the analysis of capitalistic economy.

His third step was to demonstrate that the suffering could be removed if the conditions for suffering were removed. In the fourth step he showed the new practice of life, the new social system that would be free of the suffering that the old system, of necessity, had to produce.

Freud's method of healing was essentially similar. Patients consulted Freud because they suffered and they were aware *that* they suffered. But they were usually not aware *what* they suffered *from*. The psychoanalyst's usual first task is to help patients give up their illusions about their suffering and learn what their ill-being really consists of. The diagnosis of the nature of individual or societal ill-being is a matter of interpretation, and various interpreters can differ. The patients' own picture of what they suffer from is usually the least reliable datum for a diagnosis. The essence of the psychoanalytic process is to help make patients aware of the *causes* of their ill-being.

As a consequence of such knowledge, patients can arrive at the next step: the insight that their ill-being can be cured, provided its causes are done away with. In

Freud's view this meant to lift the repression of certain infantile events. Traditional psychoanalysis seems essentially not to agree on the need for the fourth point, however. Many psychoanalysts seem to think that, by itself, insight into the repressed has a curative effect. Indeed, this is often the case, especially when the patient suffers from circumscribed symptoms, such as hysterical or obsessional symptoms. But I do not believe anything lasting can be achieved by persons who suffer from a general ill-being and for whom a change in character is necessary, *unless they change their practice of life in accordance with the change in character they want to achieve.* For instance, one can analyze the dependency of individuals until doomsday, but all the insights gained will accomplish nothing while they stay in the same practical situations they were living in before arriving at these insights. To give a simple example: a woman whose suffering is rooted in her dependency on her father, even though she has insight into deeper causes of the dependency, will not really change unless she changes her practice of life, for instance separates from her father, does not accept his favors, takes the risk and pain that these practical steps toward independence imply. *Insight separated from practice remains ineffective.*

The New Man

The function of the new society is to encourage the emergence of a new Man, beings whose character structure will exhibit the following qualities:

- Willingness to give up all forms of having, in order to fully *be.*
- Security, sense of identity, and confidence based on faith in what one *is,* on one's need for relatedness, interest, love, solidarity with the world around one, instead of on one's desire to have, to possess, to control the world, and thus become the slave of one's possessions.
- Acceptance of the fact that nobody and nothing outside oneself give meaning to life, but that this radical

independence and no-thingness can become the condition for the fullest activity devoted to caring and sharing.

- Being fully present where one is.
- Joy that comes from giving and sharing, not from hoarding and exploiting.
- Love and respect for life in all its manifestations, in the knowledge that not things, power, all that is dead, but life and everything that pertains to its growth are sacred.
- Trying to reduce greed, hate, and illusions as much as one is capable.
- Living without worshiping idols and without illusions, because one has reached a state that does not require illusions.
- Developing one's capacity for love, together with one's capacity for critical, unsentimental thought.
- Shedding one's narcissism and accepting the tragic limitations inherent in human existence.
- Making the full growth of oneself and of one's fellow beings the supreme goal of living.
- Knowing that to reach this goal, discipline and respect for reality are necessary.
- Knowing, also, that no growth is healthy that does not occur in a structure, but knowing, too, the difference between structure as an attribute of life and "order" as an attribute of no-life, of the dead.
- Developing one's imagination, not as an escape from intolerable circumstances but as the anticipation of real possibilities, as a means to do away with intolerable circumstances.
- Not deceiving others, but also not being deceived by others; one may be called innocent, but not naive.
- Knowing oneself, not only the self one knows, but also the self one does not know—even though one has a slumbering knowledge of what one does not know.
- Sensing one's oneness with all life, hence giving up the aim of conquering nature, subduing it, exploiting it, raping it, destroying it, but trying, rather, to understand and cooperate with nature.

- Freedom that is not arbitrariness but the possibility to be oneself, not as a bundle of greedy desires, but as a delicately balanced structure that at any moment is confronted with the alternative of growth or decay, life or death.
- Knowing that evil and destructiveness are necessary consequences of failure to grow.
- Knowing that only a few have reached perfection in all these qualities, but being without the ambition to "reach the goal," in the knowledge that such ambition is only another form of greed, of having.
- Happiness in the process of ever-growing aliveness, whatever the furthest point is that fate permits one to reach, for living as fully as one can is so satisfactory that the concern for what one might or might not attain has little chance to develop.

To suggest what people living in contemporary cybernetic, bureaucratic industrialism—whether in its "capitalist" or "socialist" version—could do to break through the having form of existence and to increase the being sector is not within the scope of this book. In fact, it would require a book by itself, one that might appropriately be titled "The Art of Being." But many books have been published in recent years about the road to well-being, some helpful, and many others made harmful by their fraudulence, exploiting the new market that caters to people's wish to escape their malaise. Some valuable books that might be helpful to anyone with a serious interest in the problem of achieving well-being are listed in the Bibliography.

IX

FEATURES OF THE NEW SOCIETY

A New Science of Man

The first requirement in the possible creation of the new society is to be aware of the almost insurmountable difficulties that such an attempt must face. The dim awareness of this difficulty is probably one of the main reasons that so little effort is made to make the necessary changes. Many think: "Why strive for the impossible? Let us rather act as if the course we are steering will lead us to the place of safety and happiness that our maps indicate." Those who unconsconsciously despair yet put on the mask of optimism are not necessarily wise. But those who have not given up hope can succeed only if they are hardheaded realists, shed all illusions, and fully appreciate the difficulties. This sobriety marks the distinction between *awake* and *dreaming* "utopians."

To mention only a few of the difficulties the construction of the new society has to solve:

- It would have to solve the problem of how to continue the industrial mode of production without total centralization, i.e., without ending up in fascism of the old-fashioned type or, more likely, technological "fascism with a smiling face."
- It would have to combine overall planning with a

159

high degree of decentralization, giving up the "free-market economy," that has become largely a fiction.

- It would have to give up the goal of unlimited growth for selective growth, without running the risk of economic disaster.
- It would have to create work conditions and a general spirit in which not material gain but other, psychic satisfactions are effective motivations.
- It would have to further scientific progress and, at the same time, prevent this progress from becoming a danger to the human race by its practical application.
- It would have to create conditions under which people experience well-being and joy, not the satisfaction of the maximum-pleasure drive.
- It would have to give basic security to individuals without making them dependent on a bureaucracy to feed them.
- It must restore possibilities for "individual initiative" in living, rather than in business (where it hardly exists any more anyway).

As in the development of technique some difficulties seemed insurmountable, so the difficulties listed above seem insurmountable now. But the difficulties of technique were not insurmountable because a new science had been established that proclaimed the principle of observation and knowledge of nature as conditions for controlling it (Francis Bacon: *Novum Organum,* 1620). This new science of the seventeenth century has attracted the most brilliant minds in the industrialized countries up to this day, and it led to the fulfillment of the technical Utopias the human mind had been dreaming of.

But today, roughly three and a half centuries later, we need an entirely different new science. We need a Humanistic Science of Man as the basis for the Applied Science and Art of Social Reconstruction.

Technical Utopias—flying, for example—have been achieved by the new science of nature. *The human Utopia* of the Messianic Time—a united new humankind living in solidarity and peace, free from economic determination and from war and class struggle—can be achieved, provided we spend the same energy, intelligence, and enthusiasm on the realization of the human Utopia as we have spent on the realization of our technical Utopias. One cannot construct submarines by reading Jules Verne; one cannot construct a humanist society by reading the prophets.

Whether such a change from the supremacy of natural science to a new social science will take place, nobody can tell. If it does, we might still have a chance for survival, but whether it will depends on one factor: how many brilliant, learned, disciplined, and caring men and women are attracted by the new challenge to the human mind, and by the fact that this time *the goal is not control over nature but control over technique and over irrational social forces and institutions that threaten the survival of Western society, if not of the human race.*

It is my conviction that our future depends on whether, given awareness of the present crisis, the best minds will mobilize to devote themselves to the new humanistic science of Man. For nothing short of their concerted effort will help to solve the problems already mentioned here, and to achieve the goals discussed below.

Blueprints with such general aims as "socialization of the means of production" have turned out to be socialist and communist shibboleths mainly covering up the absence of socialism. "Dictatorship of the proletariat" or of an "intellectual elite" is no less nebulous and misleading than the concept of the "free market economy" or, for that matter, of the "free" nations. Earlier socialists and communists, from Marx to Lenin, had no concrete plans for a socialist or communist society; this was the great weakness of socialism.

New social forms that will be the basis of being will not arise without many designs, models, studies, and experiments that *begin to bridge the gap between what is necessary and what is possible.* This will eventually amount to large-scale, long-run planning and to short-term proposals for first steps. The problem is the will and the humanist spirit of those who work on them; besides, when people can see a vision and simultaneously recognize what can be done step by step in a concrete way to achieve it, they will begin to feel encouragement and enthusiasm instead of fright.

If the economic and political spheres of society are to be subordinated to human development, *the model of the new society must be determined by the requirements of the unalienated, being-oriented individual.* This means that human beings shall neither live in inhuman poverty —still the main problem of the majority of people—nor be forced—as are the affluent of the industrial world—to be a *Homo consumens* by the inherent laws of capitalist production, which demand continuous growth of production and, hence, enforce growing consumption. If human beings are ever to become free and to cease feeding industry by pathological consumption, a radical change in the economic system is necessary: *we must put an end to the present situation where a healthy economy is possible only at the price of unhealthy human beings.* The task is to construct a healthy economy for healthy people.

The first crucial step toward this goal is that production shall be directed for the sake of "sane consumption."

The traditional formula "Production for *use* instead of for *profit*" is insufficient because it does not qualify what kind of use is referred to: healthy or pathological. At this point a most difficult practical question arises: Who is to determine which needs are healthy and which are pathogenic? Of one thing we can be certain: to force citizens to consume what the state decides is best—even if it *is* the best—is out of the question. Bureaucratic control that would forcibly block consumption would only make people all the more consumption hungry. Sane consumption can take place only if an ever-increasing number of people *want* to change their consumption patterns and their lifestyles. And this is possible only if people are offered a type of consumption that is more attractive than the one they are used to. This cannot happen overnight or by decree, but will require a slow educational process, and in this the government must play an important role.

The function of the state is to establish norms for healthy consumption, as against pathological and indifferent consumption. In principle, such norms can be established. The U.S. Food and Drug Administration offers a good example; it determines which foods and which drugs are harmful, basing its determination on the expert opinion of scientists in various fields, often after prolonged experimentation. In similar fashion, the value of other commodities and services can be determined by a panel of psychologists, anthropologists, sociologists, philosophers, theologians, and representatives of various social and consumer groups.

But the examination of what is life-furthering and what is life-damaging requires a depth of research that is incomparably greater than that necessary for resolving the problems of the FDA. Basic research on the nature of needs that has hardly been touched will have to be done by the new science of Man. We will need to determine which needs originate in our organism; which are the result of cultural progress; which are expressions of the individual's growth; which are synthetic, forced upon the individual by industry; which "activate" and which "passivate"; which are rooted in pathology and which in psychical health.

In contrast to the existing FDA, the decisions of the new humanist body of experts would not be implemented by force, but would serve only as guidelines, to be submitted to the citizens for discussion. We have already become very much aware of the problem of healthful and unhealthful food; the results of the experts' investigations will help to increase society's recognition of all other sane and pathological needs. People would see that most consumption engenders passivity; that the need for speed and newness, which can only be satisfied by consumerism, reflects restlessness, the inner flight from oneself; they would become aware that looking for the next thing to do or the newest gadget to use is only a means of protecting oneself from being close to oneself or to another person.

The government can greatly facilitate this educational process by subsidizing the production of desirable commodities and services, until these can be profitably produced. A large educational campaign in favor of sane consumption would have to accompany these efforts. It is to be expected that *a concerted effort to stimulate the appetite for sane consumption is likely to change the pattern of consumption*. Even if the brainwashing advertising methods that industry now uses are avoided—and this is an essential condition—it does not seem unreasonable to expect this effort to have an effect that is not too far behind that of industrial propaganda.

A standard objection to the whole program of selective consumption (and production) according to the principle of "What furthers well-being?" is that in the free market economy the consumers get precisely what they want, and hence there is no need for "selective" production. This argument is based on the assumption that consumers want what is good for them, which is, of course, blatantly untrue (in the case of drugs, or perhaps even cigarettes, nobody would use this argument). The important fact that the argument plainly ignores is that the wishes of the consumer are manufactured by the producer. In spite of competing brands, the overall effect of advertising is to stimulate the craving for consumption. All firms help each other in this basic influence via their advertising; the buyer exercises only secondarily the doubtful privilege of choosing between several competing brands. One of the standard examples offered by those who argue that the consumers' wishes are all-powerful is the failure of the Ford company's "Edsel." But the Edsel's lack of success does not alter the fact that even the advertising propaganda for it was *propaganda to buy automobiles*—from which all brands profited, except the unfortunate Edsel. Furthermore, industry influences taste by *not* producing commodities that would be more healthful to human beings but less profitable to industry.

Sane consumption is possible only if we can drastically curb the right of the stockholders and management of big enterprises to determine their production solely on the basis of profit and expansion.

Such changes could be effected by law without altering the constitutions of Western democracies (we already have many laws that restrict property rights in the interest of the public welfare). What matters is the power to direct production, not ownership of capital. In the long run, the tastes of the consumers will decide what is to be produced, once the suggestive power of advertising is ended. Either the existing enterprises will have to convert their facilities in order to satisfy the new demands, or where that is not possible, the government must spend the capital necessary for the production of new products and services that are wanted.

All these changes can only be made gradually, and with the consent of the majority of the population. But they amount to a new form of economic system, one that is as different from present-day capitalism as it is from the Soviet centralized state capitalism and from the Swedish total welfare bureaucracy.

Obviously, from the very beginning the big corporations will use their tremendous power to try to fight such changes. Only the citizens' overwhelming desire for sane consumption could break the corporations' resistance.

One effective way that citizens can demonstrate the *power of the consumer* is to build a militant consumer movement that will use the threat of "consumer strikes" as a weapon. Assume, for instance, that 20 percent of the American car-consuming population were to decide not to buy private automobiles any more, because they believed that, in comparison with excellent public transportation, the private automobile is economically wasteful, ecologically poisonous, and psychologically damaging—a drug that creates an artificial feeling of power, increases envy, and helps one to run away from oneself. While only an economist could determine how great an economic threat it would be to the automobile industry—and, of course, to the oil companies—clearly if such a consumer strike were to happen, a national economy centered around automobile production would be in serious trouble. Of course, nobody wants the American economy to be in serious trouble, but such a threat, if it can be made credible (stop using cars for one month, for instance), would give consumers a powerful leverage to induce changes in the whole system of production.

The great advantages of consumer strikes are that they do not require government action, that they are difficult to combat (unless the government were to take the step of forcing citizens to buy what they do not want to buy), and that there would be no need to wait for the accord of 51 percent of the citizens to bring enforcement by government measures. For, indeed, a 20 percent minority could be extremely effective in inducing change. Consumer strikes could cut through political lines and slogans; conservative as well as liberal and "left" humanists could participate, since one motivation would unite them all: the desire for sane and humane consumption. As the first step to calling off a consumer strike, the radical humanist consumer movement leaders would negotiate with big industry (and with the government) for the demanded changes. Their method would be basically the same as that used in negotiations to avert or end a workers' strike.

The problem in all this lies in making the consumers aware of (1) their partly unconscious protest against consumerism and (2) their potential power, once the humanist-minded consumers are organized. Such a consumers' movement would be a manifestation of genuine democracy: the individuals would express themselves directly and try to change the course of social development in an active and nonalienated fashion. And all this would be based on personal experience, not on political slogans.

But even an effective consumers' movement will not suffice as long as the power of the big corporations remains as great as it is now. For even the remnant of democracy that still exists is doomed to yield to technocratic fascism, to a society of well-fed, unthinking robots —the very type of society that was so much feared under the name of "communism"—unless the giant corporations' big hold on the government (which becomes stronger daily) and on the population (via thought control through brainwashing) is broken. The United States has a tradition of curbing the power of giant enterprises, expressed in its antitrust laws. A powerful public sentiment could move that the spirit of these laws be applied to the existing corporate superpowers, so that those superpowers would be broken up into smaller units.

To achieve a society based on being, all people must actively participate in their economic function and as citizens. Hence, our liberation from the having mode of existence is possible only through the full realization of industrial and political participatory democracy.

This demand is shared by most radical humanists.

Industrial democracy implies that each member of a large industrial or other organization plays an active role in the life of the organization; that each is fully informed and participates in decision-making, starting at the level of the individual's own work process, health and safety measures (this has already been successfully tried by a few Swedish and American enterprises) and eventually participating in decision-making at higher, general policy levels of the enterprise. It is essential that the workers and employees represent themselves, rather than be represented by trade union officials outside of the enterprise. Industrial democracy means also that the enterprise is not only an economic and technical institution, but a social institution in whose life and manner of functioning every member becomes active and, therefore, interested.

The same principles apply to the implementation of *political democracy*. Democracy can resist the authoritarian threat if it is transformed from a passive "spectator democracy" into an active "participatory democracy"—in which the affairs of the community are as close and as important to the individual citizens as their private affairs or, better, in which the well-being of the community becomes each citizen's private concern. By participating in the community, people find life becomes more interesting and stimulating. Indeed, a true political democracy can be defined as one in which life is just that, *interesting*. By its very nature such participatory democracy—in contrast to the "people's democracies" or "centralistic democracy"—is unbureaucratic and creates a climate that virtually excludes the emergence of demagogues.

Devising the methods for participatory democracy is probably far more difficult than was the elaboration of a democratic constitution in the eighteenth century. Many competent people will be required to make a gargantuan effort to devise the new principles and the implementing methods for building the participatory democracy. As just one of many possible suggestions for achieving this end, I should like to restate one I made more than twenty years ago in *The Sane Society:* that hundreds of thousands of face-to-face groups (of about five hundred members each) be created, to constitute themselves permanent bodies of deliberation and decision-making with regard to basic problems in the fields of economics, foreign policy, health, education, and the means to well-being. These groups would be given all pertinent information (the nature of this information is described later), would discuss this information (without the presence of outside influences), and would vote on the issues (and, given our current technological methods, all their votes could be collected within a day). The totality of these groups would form a "Lower House," whose decisions, along with those of other political organs, would have crucial influence on legislation.

"Why make these elaborate plans," it will be asked, "when opinion polls can perform the task of eliciting the whole population's opinion in an equally short time?" This objection touches upon one of the most problematical aspects of the expression of opinion. What is the "opinion" on which the polls are based but the views a person has without the benefit of adequate information, critical reflection, and discussion? Furthermore, the people polled know that their "opinions" do not count and, thus, have no effect. Such opinions only constitute people's conscious ideas at a given moment; they tell us nothing about the underlying trends that might lead to the opposite opinions if circumstances were to change. Similarly, the voters in a political election know that once they have voted for a candidate, they have no further real influence on the course of events. In some respects, voting in a political election is even worse than the opinion polls because of the dulling of thinking by semihypnotic techniques. Elections become an exciting soap opera, with the hopes and aspirations of the candidates—not political issues—at stake. The voters can even participate in the drama by giving their votes to the candidate with whom they side. Even though a large part of the population refuses to make this gesture, most people are fascinated by these modern Roman spectacles in which politicians, rather than gladiators, fight in the arena.

At least two requirements are involved in the formation of a genuine conviction: *adequate information and the knowledge that one's decision has an effect*. Opinions formed by the powerless onlooker do not express his or her conviction, but are a game, analogous to expressing a preference for one brand of cigarette over another. For these reasons the opinions expressed in polls and in elections constitute the worst, rather than the best, level of human judgment. This fact is confirmed by just two examples of people's best judgments, i.e., *people's decisions are far superior to the level of their political decisions* (*a*) in their private affairs (especially in business, as Joseph Schumpeter has so clearly shown) and (*b*) when they are members of juries. Juries are comprised of average citizens, who have to make decisions in cases that are often very intricate and difficult to understand. But the panel members get all pertinent information, have the chance for extended discussion, and know that their judgment decides the life and happiness of the persons they are mandated to judge. The result is that, by and large, their decisions show a great deal of insight and objectivity. In contrast, uninformed, half-hypnotized, and powerless people cannot express serious convictions. Without information, deliberation, and the power to make one's decision effective, democratically expressed opinion is hardly more than the applause at a sports event.

Active participation in political life requires maximum decentralization throughout industry and politics.

Because of the immanent logic of existing capitalism, enterprises and government grow ever larger and eventually become giants that are administered centrally from the top through a bureaucratic machine. One of the requisites of a humanistic society is that this process of centralization should stop and large-scale decentralization take place. There are several reasons for this. If a society is transformed into what Mumford has called "megamachine" (that is, if the whole of a society, including its people, is like a large, centrally directed machine), fascism is almost unavoidable in the long run because (a) people become sheep, lose their faculty for critical thinking, feel powerless, are passive, and necessarily long for a leader who "knows" what to do—and everything else *they* do not know, and (b) the "megamachine" can be put in operation by anybody with access to it, simply by pushing the proper buttons. The megamachine, like an automobile, essentially runs itself: i.e., the person behind the wheel of the car has only to push the right buttons, manage the steering and the braking, and pay some attention to a few other similarly simple details; what in a car or other machine are its many wheels, in the megamachine are the many levels of bureaucratic administration. Even a person of mediocre intelligence and ability can easily run a state once he or she is in the seat of power.

Government functions must not be delegated to states —which are themselves huge conglomerates—but to relatively small districts where people can still know and judge each other and, hence, can actively participate in the administration of their own community affairs. Decentralization in industry must give more power to small sections within a given enterprise and break up the giant corporations into small entities.

Active and responsible participation further requires that humanistic management replace bureaucratic management.

Most people still believe that every kind of large-scale administration must necessarily be "bureaucratic," i.e., an alienated form of administration. And most people are unaware of how deadening the bureaucratic spirit is and how it pervades all spheres of life, even where it seems not to be obvious, as in physician-patient and husband-wife relationships. The bureaucratic method can be defined as one that (a) administers human beings as if they were things and (b) administers things in quantitative rather than qualitative terms, in order to make quantification and control easier and cheaper. The bureaucratic method is governed by statistical data: the bureaucrats base their decisions on fixed rules arrived at from statistical data, rather than on *response to the living beings who stand before them;* they decide issues according to what is statistically most likely to be the case, at the risk of hurting the 5 or 10 percent of those who do not fit into that pattern. Bureaucrats fear personal responsibility and seek refuge behind their rules; their security and pride lie in their loyalty to rules, not in their loyalty to the laws of the human heart.

Eichmann was an extreme example of a bureaucrat. Eichmann did not send the hundreds of thousands of Jews to their deaths because he hated them; he neither hated nor loved anyone. Eichmann "did his duty": he was dutiful when he sent the Jews to their deaths; he was just as dutiful when he was charged simply with expediting their emigration from Germany. All that mattered to him was to obey the rules; he felt guilty only when he had disobeyed them. He stated (damaging his own case by this) that he felt guilty on only two counts: for having played truant as a child, and for having disobeyed orders to take shelter during an air raid. This does not imply that there was not an element of sadism in Eichmann and in many other bureaucrats, i.e., the satisfaction of controlling other living beings. But this sadistic streak is only secondary to the primary elements in bureaucrats: their lack of human response and their worship of rules.

I am not saying that all bureaucrats are Eichmanns. In the first place, many human beings in bureaucratic positions are not bureaucrats in a characterological sense. In the second place, in many cases the bureaucratic attitude has not taken over the whole person and killed his or her human side. Yet there are many Eichmanns among the bureaucrats, and the only difference is that they have not had to destroy thousands of people. But when the bureaucrat in a hospital refuses to admit a critically sick person because the rules require that the patient be sent by a physician, that bureaucrat acts no differently than Eichmann did. Neither do the social workers who decide to let a client starve, rather than violate a certain rule in their bureaucratic code. This bureaucratic attitude exists not only among administrators; it lives among physicians, nurses, schoolteachers, professors—as well as in many husbands in relation to their wives and in many parents in relation to their children.

Once the living human being is reduced to a number, the true bureaucrats can commit acts of utter cruelty, not because they are driven by cruelty of a magnitude commensurate to their deeds, but because they feel no human bond to their subjects. While less vile than pure sadists, the bureaucrats are more dangerous, because in them there is not even a conflict between conscience and duty: their conscience *is* doing their duty; human beings as objects of empathy and compassion do not exist for them.

The old-fashioned bureaucrat, who was prone to be unfriendly, still exists in some old-established enterprises or in such large organizations as welfare departments, hospitals, and prisons, in which a single bureaucrat has considerable power over poor or otherwise powerless people. The bureaucrats in modern industry are not unfriendly and probably have little of the sadistic streak, even though they may get some pleasure from having power over people. But again, we find in them that bureaucratic allegiance to a thing—in their case, the *system*: they believe in *it*. The corporation is their home, and its rules are sacred because the rules are "rational."

But neither the old nor the new bureaucrats can coexist in a system of participatory democracy, for the bureaucratic spirit is incompatible with the spirit of active participation by the individual. The new social scientists must devise plans for new forms of nonbureaucratic large-scale administration that is directed by response (that reflects "responsibility") to people and situations rather than by the mere application of rules. Nonbureaucratic administration *is* possible provided we take into account the potential spontaneity of response in the administrator and do not make a fetish of economizing.

Success in establishing a society of being depends on many other measures. In offering the following suggestions, I make no claim to originality; on the contrary, I am encouraged by the fact that almost all of these suggestions have been made in one form or another by humanist writers.*

- *All brainwashing methods in industrial and political advertising must be prohibited.*

These brainwashing methods are dangerous not only because they impel us to buy things that we neither need nor want, but because they lead us to choose political representatives we would neither need nor want *if* we were in full control of our minds. But we are *not* in full control of our minds because hypnoid methods are used to propagandize us. To combat this ever-increasing danger, *we must prohibit the use of all hypnoid forms of propaganda, for commodities as well as for politicians.*

The hypnoid methods used in advertising and political propaganda are a serious danger to mental health, specifically to clear and critical thinking and emotional independence. I have no doubt that thorough studies will show that the damage caused by drug addiction is only a fraction of the damage done by our methods of brainwashing, from subliminal suggestions to such semihypnotic devices as constant repetition or the deflection of rational thought by the appeal to sexual lust ("I'm Linda, fly me!"). The bombardment with purely suggestive methods in advertising, and most of all in television commercials, is stultifying. This assault on reason and the sense of reality pursues the individual everywhere and daily at any time: during many hours of watching television, or when driving on a highway, or in the political propaganda of candidates, and so on. The particular effect of these suggestive methods is that they create an atmosphere of being half-awake, of believing and not believing, of losing one's sense of reality.

Stopping the poison of mass suggestion will have a withdrawal effect on consumers that will be little different from the withdrawal symptoms drug addicts experience when they stop taking drugs.

*In order not to overburden this book I refrain from quoting the large literature that contains similar proposals. Many titles may be found in the Bibliography.

• *The gap between the rich and the poor nations must
be closed.*

There is little doubt that the continuation and further
deepening of that gap will lead to catastrophe. The poor
nations have ceased to accept the economic exploitation
by the industrial world as a God-given fact. Even though
the Soviet Union is still exploiting its own satellite states
in the same colonialist manner, it uses and reinforces the
protest of the colonial peoples as a political weapon
against the West. The increase in oil prices was the
beginning—and a symbol—of the colonial peoples' demand to end the system that requires them to sell raw
materials cheap and buy industrial products dear. In the
same way, the Vietnam war was a symbol of the beginning of the end of the colonial peoples' political and
military domination by the West.

What will happen if nothing crucial is done to close
the gap? Either epidemics will spread into the fortress of
the white society or famines will drive the population of
the poor nations into such despair that they, perhaps
with the help of sympathizers from the industrial world,
will commit acts of destruction, even use small nuclear or
biological weapons, that will bring chaos within the white
fortress.

This catastrophic possibility can be averted only if the
conditions of hunger, starvation, and sickness are brought
under control—and to do that, the help of the industrial
nations is vitally necessary. The methods for such help
must be free from all interests in profits and political
advantages on the side of the rich countries; this means
also that they must be free from the idea that the economic and political principles of capitalism are to be
transferred to Africa and Asia. Obviously, *the* most effi-
cient way for economic help to be given is a matter for
economic experts to determine.

But only those who can qualify as true experts can
serve this cause, individuals who have not only brilliant
brains but humane hearts that impel them to seek the
optimal solution. In order for these experts to be called
in, and their recommendations to be followed, the having

orientation must greatly weaken, and a sense of solidarity, of caring (not of pity) must emerge. Caring means caring not only for our fellow beings on this earth but also for our descendants. Indeed, nothing is more telling about our selfishness than that we go on plundering the raw materials of the earth, poisoning the earth, and preparing nuclear war. We hesitate not at all at leaving our own descendants this plundered earth as their heritage.

Will this inner transformation take place? No one knows. But one thing the world should know is that without it the clash between poor and rich nations will become unmanageable.

- *Many of the evils of present-day capitalist and communist societies would disappear with the introduction of a guaranteed yearly income.**

The core of this idea is that all persons, regardless of whether they work or not, shall have the unconditional right not to starve and not to be without shelter. They shall receive not more than is basically required to sustain themselves—but neither shall they receive less. This right expresses a new concept for today, though a very old norm, demanded by Christianity and practiced in many "primitive" tribes, that human beings have an *unconditional right to live, regardless of whether they do their "duty to society."* It is right we guarantee to our pets, but not to our fellow beings.

The realm of personal freedom would be tremendously enlarged by such a law; no person who is economically dependent on another (e.g., on a parent, husband, boss) could any longer be forced to submit to the blackmail of starvation; gifted persons wanting to prepare for a different life could do so provided they were willing to make the sacrifice of living in a degree of poverty for a time. Modern welfare states have accepted this principle— almost . . . which actually means "not really." A bureaucracy still "administers" the people, still controls and

---

*I proposed this in 1955 in *The Sane Society;* the same proposal was made in a mid-1960s symposium (edited by A. Theobald; see Bibliography).

humiliates them. But a guaranteed income would require no "proof" of need for any person to get a simple room and a minimum of food. Thus no bureaucracy would be needed to administer a welfare program with its inherent waste and its violations of human dignity.

The guaranteed yearly income would ensure real freedom and independence. For that reason, it is unacceptable to any system based on exploitation and control, particularly the various forms of dictatorship. It is characteristic of the Soviet system that even suggestions for the simplest forms of free goods (for example, free public transportation or free milk) have been consistently rejected. Free medical service is the exception, but only apparently so, since here the free service is in response to a clear condition: one must be sick to receive it.

Considering the present-day cost of running a large welfare bureaucracy, the cost of treating physical, especially psychosomatic, illnesses, criminality, and drug addiction (all of which are largely forms of protest against coercion and boredom), it seems likely that the cost of providing any person who wanted it with a guaranteed annual income would be less than that of our present system of social welfare. The idea will appear unfeasible or dangerous to those who believe that "people are basically lazy by nature." This chiché has no basis in fact, however; it is simply a slogan that serves as a rationalization for the resistance against surrendering the sense of power over those who are helpless.

- *Women must be liberated from patriarchal domination.*

The freedom of women from patriarchal domination is a fundamental factor in the humanization of society. The domination of women by men began only about six thousand years ago in various parts of the world when surplus in agriculture permitted the hiring and exploitation of workers, the organization of armies, and the building of powerful city-states.* Since then, not only Middle Eastern

*I have discussed the early "matriarchate" and the literature related to it in *The Anatomy of Human Destructiveness.*

and European societies but most of the world's cultures have been conquered by the "associated males" who subdued the women. This victory of the male over the female of the human species was based on the men's economic power and the military machine they built.

The war between the sexes is as old as the war between the classes, but its forms are more complicated, since men have needed women not only as working beasts but also as mothers, lovers, solace-givers. The forms of the war between the sexes are often overt and brutal, more often hidden. Women yielded to superior force, but fought back with their own weapons, their chief one being ridicule of the men.

The subjugation of one half of the human race by the other has done, and still does, immense harm to both sexes: the men assume the characteristics of the victor, the women those of the victim. No relation between a man and a woman, even today, and even among those who consciously protest against male supremacy, is free from the curse either, among men, of feeling superior or, among women, of feeling inferior. (Freud, the unquestioning believer in male superiority, unfortunately assumed that women's sense of powerlessness was due to their alleged regret that they have no penis, and that men were insecure because of their alleged universal "fear of castration." What we are dealing with in this phenomenon are symptoms of the war between the sexes, not biological and anatomical differences as such.)

Many data show how much men's control over women resembles one group's control over other powerless populations. As an example, consider the similarity between the picture of the blacks in the American South a hundred years ago and that of women at that time, and even up to today. Blacks and women were compared to children; they were supposed to be emotional, naive, without a sense of reality, so that they were not to be trusted with making decisions; they were supposed to be irresponsible, but charming. (Freud added to the catalogue that women had a less developed conscience [superego] than men and were more narcissistic.)

The exercise of power over those who are weaker is the

essence of existing patriarchy, as it is the essence of the
domination of nonindustrialized nations and of children
and adolescents. The growing movement for women's
liberation is of enormous significance because it is a
threat to the principle of power on which contemporary
society (capitalist and communist alike) lives—that is, if
the women clearly mean by liberation that they do not
want to share the men's power over other groups, such as
the power over the colonial peoples. If the movement for
the liberation of women can identify its own role and
function as representative of "antipower," women will
have a decisive influence in the battle for a new society.

Basic liberating changes have already been made. Perhaps a later historian will report that the most revolutionary event in the twentieth century was the beginning of
women's liberation and the downfall of men's supremacy.
But the fight for the liberation of women has only just
begun, and men's resistance cannot be overestimated.
Their whole relation to women (including their sexual
relation) has been based on their alleged superiority, and
they have already begun to feel quite uncomfortable and
anxious vis-à-vis those women who refuse to accept the
myth of male superiority.

Closely related to the women's liberation movement is
the antiauthoritarian turn of the younger generations.
This antiauthoritarianism had its peak in the late sixties;
now, through a number of changes, many of the rebels
against the "establishment" have essentially become
"good" again. But the starch has nonetheless been
washed out of the old worship of parental and other
authorities, and it seems certain that the old "awe" of
authority will not return.

Paralleling this emancipation from authority is the liberation from guilt about sex: sex certainly seems to have
ceased being unspeakable and sinful. However people
may differ in their opinions regarding the relative merits
of the many facets of the sexual revolution, one thing is
sure: sex no longer frightens people; it can no longer be
used to develop a sense of guilt, and thereby to force
submission.

- *A Supreme Cultural Council, charged with the task of advising the government, the politicians, and the citizens in all matters in which knowledge is necessary, should be established.*

The cultural council members would be representative of the intellectual and artistic elite of the country, men and women whose integrity was beyond doubt. They would determine the composition of the new, expanded form of the FDA and would select the people to be responsible for disseminating information.

There is a substantial consensus on who the outstanding representatives of various branches of culture are, and I believe it would be possible to find the right members for such a council. It is of decisive importance, of course, that this council should also represent those who are opposed to established views: for instance, the "radicals" and "revisionists" in economics, history, and sociology. The difficulty is not in *finding* the council members but in *choosing* them, for they cannot be elected by popular vote, nor should they be appointed by the government. Yet other ways of selecting them may be found. For instance, start with a nucleus of three or four persons and gradually enlarge the group to its full size of, say, fifty to a hundred persons. This cultural council should be amply financed so that it would be able to commission special studies of various problems.

- *A system of effective dissemination of effective information must also be established.*

Information is a crucial element in the formation of an effective democracy. Withholding information or falsifying it in the alleged interests of "national security" must be ended. But even without such illegitimate withholding of information, the problem remains that at present the amount of real and necessary information given to the average citizen is almost zero. And this holds true not only for the average citizen. As has been shown abundantly, most elected representatives, members of government, leaders of the defense forces, and business leaders are badly informed and to a large extent misinformed by the falsehoods that various government agencies spread, and the news media repeat. Unfortunately, most of these same people, in turn, have at best a purely manipulative intelligence. They have little capacity to understand the forces operating beneath the surface and, hence, to make sound judgments about future developments, not to speak of their selfishness and dishonesty, of which we have heard enough. But even to be an honest and intelligent bureaucrat is not enough to solve the problems of a world facing catastrophe.

With the exception of a few "great" newspapers, even the factual information on political, economic, and social data is extremely limited. The so-called great newspapers inform better, but they also misinform better: by not publishing all the news impartially; by slanting headlines, in addition to writing headlines that often do not conform with their accompanying text; by being partisan in their editorials, written under the cover of seemingly reasonable and moralizing language. In fact, the newspapers, the magazines, television, and radio produce a commodity: *news,* from the raw material of events. Only news is salable, and the news media determine which events are news, which are not. At the very best, information is ready-made, concerns only the surface of events, and barely gives the citizens an opportunity to penetrate through the surface and recognize the deeper causes of the events. As long as the sale of news is a business, newspapers and magazines can hardly be prevented from printing what sells (in various degrees of unscrupulousness) their publications and does not antagonize the advertisers.

The information problem must be solved in a different way if informed opinion and decision are to be possible. As an example of such a way I mention only one: that one of the first and most important functions of the Supreme Cultural Council would be to gather and disseminate all the information that would serve the needs of the whole population and, particularly, would serve as the basis for discussion among the face-to-face groups in our participatory democracy. This information should contain basic facts and basic alternatives in all areas in which political decisions take place. It is of special importance that in case of disagreement the minority opinion *and* the majority opinion would be published, and that this information would be made available to every citizen and particularly to the face-to-face groups. The Supreme Cultural Council would be responsible for supervising the work of this new body of news reporters, and, of course, radio and television would have an important role in disseminating this kind of information.

- *Scientific research must be separated from application in industry and defense.*

While it would be hobbling of human development if one set any limits to the demand for knowledge, it would be extremely dangerous if practical use were made of all the results of scientific thinking. As has been emphasized by many observers, certain discoveries in genetics, in brain surgery, in psychodrugs, and in many other areas can and will be misused to the great damage of Man. This is unavoidable as long as industrial and military interests are free to make use of all new theoretical discoveries as they see fit. Profit and military expediency must cease to determine the application of scientific research. This will require a control board, whose permission would be necessary for the practical application of any new theoretical discovery. Needless to say, such a control board must be—legally and psychologically—completely independent of industry, the government, and the military. The Supreme Cultural Council would have the authority to appoint and supervise this control board.

- While all the suggestions made in the foregoing pages will be difficult enough to realize, our difficulties become almost insurmountable with the addition of another necessary condition of a new society: *atomic disarmament.*

One of the sick elements in our economy is that it needs a large armament industry. Even today, the United States, the richest country in the world, must curtail its expenses for health, welfare, and education in order to carry the load of its defense budget. The cost of social experimentation cannot possibly be borne by a state that is making itself poor by the production of hardware that is useful only as a means of suicide. Furthermore, the spirit of individualism and activity cannot live in an atmosphere where the military bureaucracy, gaining in power every day, continues to further fear and subordination.

The New Society: Is There a Reasonable Chance?

Considering the power of the corporations, the apathy and powerlessness of the large mass of the population, the inadequacy of political leaders in almost all countries, the threat of nuclear war, the ecological dangers, not to speak of such phenomena as weather changes that alone could produce famines in large parts of the world, *is there a reasonable chance for salvation?* From the standpoint of a business deal, there is no such chance; no reasonable human beings would bet their fortunes when the odds represent only a 2 percent chance of winning, or make a large investment of capital in a business venture with the same poor chance of gain. But when it is a matter of life and death, "reasonable chance" must be translated into "real possibility," however small it may be.

Life is neither a game of chance nor a business deal, and we must seek elsewhere for an appreciation of the real possibilities for salvation: in the healing art of medicine, for example. If a sick person has even the barest chance for survival, no responsible physician will say, "Let's give up the effort," or will use only palliatives. On the contrary, everything conceivable is done to save the sick person's life. Certainly, a sick society cannot expect anything less.

Judging present-day society's chances for salvation from the standpoint of betting or business rather than from the standpoint of life is characteristic of the spirit of a business society. There is little wisdom in the currently fashionable technocratic view that there is nothing seriously wrong in keeping ourselves busy with work or fun, in not feeling, and that even *if* there is, perhaps technocratic fascism may not be so bad, after all. But this is wishful thinking. Technocratic fascism must necessarily lead to catastrophe. Dehumanized Man will become so mad that he will not be able to sustain a viable society in the long run, and in the short run will not be able to refrain from the suicidal use of nuclear or biological weapons.

Yet there are a few factors that can give us some encouragement. The first is that a growing number of people now recognize the truth that Mesarovic and Pestel, Ehrlich and Ehrlich, and others have stated: that *on purely economic grounds* a new ethic, a new attitude toward nature, human solidarity, and cooperation are necessary if the Western world is not to be wiped out. This appeal to reason, even aside from any emotional and ethical considerations, may mobilize the minds of not a few people. It should not be taken lightly, even though, historically, nations have again and again acted against their vital interests and even against the drive for survival. They could do so because the people were persuaded by their leaders that the choice between "to be or not to be" did not confront them. Had they recognized the truth, however, the normal neurophysiological reaction would have taken place: their awareness of vital threats would have mobilized appropriate defense action.

Another hopeful sign is the increasing display of dissatisfaction with our present social system. A growing number of people feel *le malaise du siècle:* they sense their depression; they are conscious of it, in spite of all kinds of efforts to repress it. They feel the unhappiness of their isolation and the emptiness of their "togetherness"; they feel their impotence, the meaninglessness of their lives. Many feel all this very clearly and consciously; others feel it less clearly, but are fully aware of it when someone else puts it into words.

So far in world history a life of empty pleasure was possible for only a small elite, and they remained essentially sane because they knew they had power and that they had to think and to act in order not to lose their power. Today, the empty life of consumption is that of the whole middle class, which economically and politically has no power and little personal responsibility. The major part of the Western world knows the benefits of the consumer type of happiness, and growing numbers of those who benefit from it are finding it wanting. They are beginning to discover that having much does not create well-being: traditional ethical teaching has been put to the test—and is being confirmed by experience.

Only in those who live without the benefits of middle-class luxury does the old illusion remain untouched: in the lower middle classes in the West and among the vast majority in the "socialist" countries. Indeed, the bourgeois hope for "happiness through consumption" is nowhere more alive than in the countries that have not yet fulfilled the bourgeois dream.

One of the gravest objections to the possibilities of overcoming greed and envy, namely that their strength is inherent in human nature, loses a good deal of its weight upon further examination. Greed and envy are so strong not because of their *inherent intensity* but because of the difficulty in resisting the public pressure to be a wolf with the wolves. Change the social climate, the values that are either approved or disapproved, and the change from selfishness to altruism will lose most of its difficulty.

Thus we arrive again at the premise that the being orientation is a strong potential in human nature. Only a minority is governed by the having mode, while another small minority is governed by the being mode. Either can become dominant, and which one does depends on the social structure. In a society oriented mainly toward being, the having tendencies are starved and the being mode is fed. In a society like ours, whose main orientation is toward having, the reverse occurs. But the being mode of existence is always already present—though repressed. No Saul becomes a Paul if he was not already a Paul before his conversion.

The change from having to being is actually a tipping of the scales, when in connection with social change the new is encouraged and the old discouraged. Besides, this is not a question of a new Man as different from the old as the sky is from the earth; it is a question of a change of direction. One step in the new direction will be followed by the next, and taken in the right direction, these steps mean everything.

Yet another encouraging aspect to consider is one that, paradoxically, concerns the degree of alienation that characterizes the majority of the population, including its leaders. As pointed out in the earlier discussion of the "marketing character," the greed to have and to hoard has been modified by the tendency to merely function well, to exchange oneself as a commodity who is—nothing. It is easier for the alienated, marketing character to change than it is for the hoarding character, which is frantically holding onto possessions, and particularly its ego.

A hundred years ago, when the major part of the population consisted of "independents," the greatest obstacle to change was the fear of and resistance to loss of property and economic independence. Marx lived at a time when the working class was the only large dependent class and, as Marx thought, the most alienated one. Today, the vast majority of the population is *dependent;* virtually all people who work are *employed* (according to the 1970 U.S. Census report, only 7.82 percent of the total working population over age sixteen is self-employed, i.e., "independent"); and—at least in the United States—it is the blue-collar workers who still maintain the traditional middle-class hoarding character, and who, consequently, are less open to change than is today's more alienated middle class.

All this has a most important political consequence: while socialism was striving for the liberation of all classes—i.e., striving for a classless society—its immediate appeal was to the "working class," i.e., the manual workers; today the working class is (in relative terms) even more of a minority than it was a hundred years ago. In order to gain power, the social democratic parties need to win the votes of many members of the middle class, and in order to achieve this goal, the socialist parties have had to cut back their program from one with a socialist vision to one offering liberal reforms. On the other hand, by identifying the working class as the lever of humanistic change, socialism necessarily antagonized the members of all other classes, who felt that their properties and privileges were going to be taken away by the workers.

Today, the appeal of the new society goes to all who suffer from alienation, who are employed, and whose property is not threatened. In other words, it concerns the majority of the population, not merely a minority. It does not threaten to take anybody's property, and as far as income is concerned, it would raise the standard of living of those who are poor. High salaries for top executives would not have to be lowered, but if the system worked, they would not want to be symbols of times past.

Furthermore, the ideals of the new society cross all party lines: many conservatives have not lost their ethical and religious ideals (Eppler calls them "value conservatives"), and the same holds true of many liberals and leftists. Each political party exploits the voters by persuading them that it represents the true values of humanism. Yet behind all political parties are only two camps: *those who care and those who don't care.* If all those in the camp that cares could rid themselves of party clichés and realize that they have the same goals, the possibility of change would seem to be considerably greater; especially so since most citizens have become less and less interested in party loyalty and party slogans. People today are yearning for human beings who have wisdom and convictions and the courage to act according to their convictions.

Given even these hopeful factors, however, the chances for necessary human and social changes remain slim. Our only hope lies in the energizing attraction of a new vision. To propose this or that reform that does not change the system is useless in the long run because it does not carry with it the impelling force of a strong motivation. The "utopian" goal is more realistic than the "realism" of today's leaders. The realization of the new society and new Man is possible only if the old motivations of profit and power are replaced by new ones: being, sharing, understanding; if the marketing character is replaced by the productive, loving character; if cybernetic religion is replaced by a new radical-humanistic spirit.

Indeed, for those who are not authentically rooted in

theistic religion the crucial question is that of conversion to a humanistic "religiosity" without religion, without dogmas and institutions, a "religiosity" long prepared by the movement of nontheistic religiosity, from the Buddha to Marx. We are not confronted with the choice between selfish materialism and the acceptance of the Christian concept of God. Social life itself—in all its aspects in work, in leisure, in personal relations—will be the expression of the "religious" spirit, and no separate religion will be necessary. This demand for a new, nontheistic, noninstitutionalized "religiosity" is not an attack on the existing religions. It does mean, however, that the Roman Catholic Church, beginning with the Roman bureaucracy, must convert *itself* to the spirit of the gospel. It does not mean that the "socialist countries" must be "desocialized," but that their fake socialism shall be replaced by genuine humanistic socialism.

Later Medieval culture flourished because people followed the vision of the *City of God.* Modern society flourished because people were energized by the vision of the growth of the *Earthly City of Progress.* In our century, however, this vision deteriorated to that of the *Tower of Babel,* which is now beginning to collapse and will ultimately bury everybody in its ruins. If the City of God and the Earthly City were *thesis* and *antithesis,* a new *synthesis* is the only alternative to chaos: the synthesis between the spiritual core of the Late Medieval world and the development of rational thought and science since the Renaissance. This synthesis is *The City of Being.*

Bibliography

Included in the Bibliography are all books cited in the text, although not all sources used in the preparation of this work. Books especially recommended for collateral reading are marked with a single asterisk; a second asterisk denotes books for readers with limited time.

AQUINAS, THOMAS. 1953. *Summa Theologica.* Edited by P. H. M. Christmann. OP. Heidelberg: Gemeinschaftsverlage, F. H. Kerle; Graz: A. Pustet.

ARIETI, SILVANO, ed. 1959. *American Handbook of Psychiatry,* vol. 2. New York: Basic Books.

ARISTOTLE. *Nicomachean Ethics.* Cambridge: Harvard University Press, Loeb Classical Library.

*ARTZ, FREDERICK B. 1959. *The Mind of the Middle Ages: An Historical Survey: A.D. 200–1500.* 3rd rev. ed. New York: Alfred A. Knopf.

AUER, ALFONS. "Die Autonomie des Sittlichen nach Thomas von Aquin" [The anatomy of ethics according to Thomas Aquinas]. Unpublished paper.

————. 1975. "Ist die Sünde eine Beleidigung Gottes?" [Is sin an insult to God?]. In *Theol. Quartalsschrift.* Munich, Freiberg: Erich Wewel Verlag.

*————. 1976. *Utopie, Technologie, Lebensqualität* [Utopia, technology, quality of life]. Zurich: Benziger Verlag.

*BACHOFEN, J. J. 1967. *Myth, Religion and the Mother Right: Selected Writings of Johann Jakob Bachofen.* Edited by J. Campbell; translated by R. Manheim. Princeton: Princeton University Press. (Original ed. *Das Mutterrecht,* 1861.)

BACON, FRANCIS. 1620. *Novum Organum.*

BAUER, E. *Allgemeine Literatur Zeitung 1843/4.* Quoted by K. Marx and F. Engels; q.v.

*BECKER, CARL L. 1932. *The Heavenly City of the Eighteenth Century Philosophers.* New Haven: Yale University Press.

BENVENISTE, EMILE. 1966. *Problèmes de Linguistique Général.* Paris: Ed. Gallimard.

BENZ, E. See Eckhart, Meister.

BLAKNEY, RAYMOND B. See Eckhart, Meister.

BLOCH, ERNST. 1970. *Philosophy of the Future.* New York: Seabury Press.

————. 1971. *On Karl Marx.* New York: Seabury Press.

*————. 1972. *Atheism in Christianity.* New York: Seabury Press.

Cloud of Unknowing, The. See Underhill, Evelyn.

DARWIN, CHARLES. 1969. *The Autobiography of Charles Darwin 1809–1882.* Edited by Nora Barlow. New York: W. W. Norton. Quoted by E. F. Schumacher; q.v.

DELGADO, J. M. R. 1967. "Aggression and Defense Under Cerebral Radio Control." In *Aggression and Defense: Neural Mechanisms and Social Patterns. Brain Function,* vol. 5. Edited by C. D. Clemente and D. B. Lindsley. Berkeley: University of California Press.

DE LUBAC, HENRI. 1943. *Katholizismus als Gemeinschaft.* Translated by Hans-Urs von Balthasar. Einsiedeln/Cologne: Verlag Benziger & Co.

DE MAUSE, LLOYD, ed. 1974. *The History of Childhood.* New York: The Psychohistory Press, Atcom Inc.

DIOGENES LAERTIUS. 1966. In *Lives of Eminent Philosophers.* Translated by R. D. Hicks. Cambridge: Harvard University Press.

DU MARAIS. 1769. *Les Véritables Principes de la Grammaire.*

DUMOULIN, HEINRICH. 1966. *Östliche Meditation und Christliche Mystik.* Freiburg/Munich: Verlag Karl Alber.

**ECKHART, MEISTER. 1941. *Meister Eckhart: A Modern Translation.* Translated by Raymond B. Blakney. New York: Harper & Row, Torchbooks.

————. 1950. Edited by Franz Pfeifer; translated by C. de B. Evans. London: John M. Watkins.

————. 1969. *Meister Eckhart, Deutsche Predigten und Traktate.* Edited and translated by Joseph L. Quint. Munich: Carl Hanser Verlag.

————. *Meister Eckhart, Die Deutschen Werke.* Edited and translated by Joseph L. Quint. In *Gesamtausgabe der deutschen und lateinischen Werke.* Stuttgart: Kohlhammer Verlag.

————. *Meister Eckhart, Die lateinischen Werke, Expositio Exodi 16.* Edited by E. Benz et al. In *Gesamtausgabe der deutschen und lateinischen Werke.* Stuttgart: Kohlhammer Verlag. Quoted by Otto Schilling; q.v.

*EHRLICH, PAUL R., and EHRLICH, ANNE H. 1970. *Population, Re-*

sources, *Environment: Essays in Human Ecology*. San Francisco: W. H. Freeman.

ENGELS, F. See Marx, K., jt. auth.

EPPLER, E. 1975. *Ende oder Wende* [End or change]. Stuttgart: W. Kohlhammer Verlag.

FARNER, KONRAD. 1947. "Christentum und Eigentum bis Thomas von Aquin." In *Mensch und Gesellschaft*, vol. 12. Edited by K. Farner. Bern: Francke Verlag. Quoted by Otto Schilling; q.v.

FINKELSTEIN, LOUIS. 1946. *The Pharisees: The Sociological Background of Their Faith*, vols. 1, 2. Philadelphia: The Jewish Publication Society of America.

FROMM, E. 1932. "Die psychoanalytische Charakterologie und ihre Bedeutung für die Sozialforschung." *Ztsch. f. Sozialforschung*. 1: 253–277. "Psychoanalytic Characterology and Its Relevance for Social Psychology." In E. Fromm, *The Crisis of Psychoanalysis;* q.v.

——. 1941. *Escape from Freedom*. New York: Holt, Rinehart and Winston.

——. 1942. "Faith as a Character Trait." In *Psychiatry 5*. Reprinted with slight changes in E. Fromm, *Man for Himself;* q.v.

——. 1943. "Sex and Character." In *Psychiatry 6*: 21–31. Reprinted in E. Fromm, *The Dogma of Christ and Other Essays on Religion, Psychology, and Culture;* q.v.

*——. 1947. *Man for Himself: An Inquiry into the Psychology of Ethics*. New York: Holt, Rinehart and Winston.

——. 1950. *Psychoanalysis and Religion*. New Haven: Yale University Press.

——. 1951. *The Forgotten Language: An Introduction to the Understanding of Dreams, Fairy Tales, and Myths*. New York: Holt, Rinehart and Winston.

*——. 1955. *The Sane Society*. New York: Holt, Rinehart and Winston.

——. 1956. *The Art of Loving*. New York: Harper & Row.

——. 1959. "On the Limitations and Dangers of Psychology." In W. Leibrecht, ed. *Religion and Culture: Essays in Honor of Paul Tillich;* q.v.

**——. 1961. *Marx's Concept of Man*. New York: Frederick Ungar.

——. 1963. *The Dogma of Christ and Other Essays on Religion, Psychology, and Culture*. New York: Holt, Rinehart and Winston.

——. 1964. *The Heart of Man*. New York: Harper & Row.

——, ed. 1965. *Socialist Humanism*. Garden City, N.Y.: Doubleday & Co.

——. 1966. "The Concept of Sin and Repentance." In E. Fromm, *You Shall Be as Gods;* q.v.

————. 1966. *You Shall Be as Gods.* New York: Holt, Rinehart and Winston.

*————. 1968. *The Revolution of Hope.* New York: Harper & Row.

————. 1970. *The Crisis of Psychoanalysis: Essays on Freud, Marx, and Social Psychology.* New York: Holt, Rinehart and Winston.

**————. 1973. *The Anatomy of Human Destructiveness.* New York: Holt, Rinehart and Winston.

————, and Maccoby, M. 1970. *Social Character in a Mexican Village.* Englewood Cliffs, N.J.: Prentice-Hall.

————. Suzuki, D. T., and de Martino, R. 1960. *Zen Buddhism and Psychoanalysis.* New York: Harper & Row.

*GALBRAITH, JOHN KENNETH. 1969. *The Affluent Society.* 2nd ed. Boston: Houghton Mifflin.

*————. 1971. *The New Industrial Society.* 2nd rev. ed. Boston: Houghton Mifflin.

*————. 1974. *Economics and the Public Purpose.* Boston: Houghton Mifflin.

*HABERMAS, JÜRGEN. 1971. *Toward a Rational Society.* Translated by J. Schapiro. Boston: Beacon Press.

————. 1973. *Theory and Practice.* Edited by J. Viertel. Boston: Beacon Press.

HARICH, W. 1975. *Kommunismus ohne Wachstum.* Hamburg: Rowohlt Verlag.

HEBB, D. O. "Drives and the CNS [Conceptual Nervous System]." *Psych. Rev.* 62, 4: 244.

HESS, MOSES. 1843. "Philosophie der Tat" [The philosophy of action]. In *Einundzwanzig Bogen aus der Schweiz.* Edited by G. Herewegh. Zurich: Literarischer Comptoir. Reprinted in Moses Hess, *Ökonomische Schriften.* Edited by D. Horster. Darmstadt: Melzer Verlag, 1972.

*ILLICH, IVAN. 1970. *Deschooling Society.* World Perspectives, vol. 44. New York: Harper & Row.

————. 1976. *Medical Nemesis: The Expropriation of Health.* New York: Pantheon.

*KROPOTKIN, P. A. 1902. *Mutual Aid: A Factor of Evolution.* London.

LANGE, WINFRIED. 1969. *Glückseligkeitsstreben und uneigennützige Lebensgestaltung bei Thomas von Aquin.* Diss. Freiburg im Breisgau.

LEIBRECHT, W., ed. 1959. *Religion and Culture: Essays in Honor of Paul Tillich.* New York: Harper & Row.

LOBKOWICZ, NICHOLAS. 1967. *Theory and Practice: The History of a Concept from Aristotle to Marx.* International Studies Series. Notre Dame, Ind.: University of Notre Dame Press.

*MACCOBY, MICHAEL. Forthcoming, fall 1976. *The Gamesmen: The New Corporate Leaders*. New York: Simon and Schuster.

MAIMONIDES, MOSES. 1963. *The Code of Maimonides*. Translated by A. M. Hershman. New Haven: Yale University Press.

*MARCEL, GABRIEL. 1965. *Being and Having: An Existentialist Diary*. New York: Harper & Row, Torchbooks.

MARX, K. 1844. *Economic and Philosophical Manuscripts*. In *Gesamtausgabe (MEGA)* [Complete works of Marx and Engels]. Moscow. Translated by E. Fromm in E. Fromm, *Marx's Concept of Man*; q.v.

―――. 1909. *Capital*. Chicago: Charles H. Kerr & Co.

―――. *Grundrisse der Kritik der politischen Ökonomie*. [Outline of the critique of political economy]. Frankfurt: Europaische Verlagsanstalt, n.d. McClellan, David, ed. and trans. 1971. *The Grundrisse*, Excerpts. New York: Harper & Row, Torchbooks.

―――, and ENGELS, F. 1844/5. *The Holy Family, or a Critique of Critical Critique*. London: Lawrence & Wishart, 1957. *Die Heilige Familie, der Kritik der kritischen Kritik*. Berlin: Dietz Verlag, 1971.

MAYO ELTON. 1933. *The Human Problems of an Industrial Civilization*. New York: Macmillan.

MEADOWS, D. H., et al. 1972. *The Limits to Growth*. New York: Universe Books.

*MESAROVIC, MIHAJLO D., and PESTEL, EDUARD. 1974. *Mankind at the Turning Point*. New York: E. P. Dutton.

MIETH, DIETMAR. 1969. *Die Einheit von Vita Activa und Vita Contemplativa*. Regensburg: Verlag Friedrich Pustet.

―――. 1971. *Christus—Das Soziale im Menschen*. Düsseldorf: Topos Taschenbücher, Patmos Verlag.

MILL, J. S. 1965. *Principles of Political Economy*. 7th ed., reprint of 1871 ed. Toronto: University of Toronto/Routledge and Kegan Paul.

MILLAN, IGNACIO. Forthcoming. *The Character of Mexican Executives*.

MORGAN, L. H. 1870. *Systems of Sanguinity and Affinity of the Human Family*. Publication 218, Washington, D.C.: Smithsonian Institution.

**MUMFORD, L. 1970. *The Pentagon of Power*. New York: Harcourt Brace Jovanovich.

**NYANAPONIKA MAHATERA. 1962; 1970. *The Heart of Buddhist Meditation*. London: Rider & Co.; New York: Samuel Weiser.

*―――, ed. 1971; 1972. *Pathways of Buddhist Thought: Essays from the Wheel*. London: George Allen & Unwin; New York: Barnes & Noble, Harper & Row.

PHELPS, EDMUND S., ed. 1975. *Altruism, Morality and Economic Theory*. New York: Russell Sage Foundation.

PIAGET, JEAN. 1932. *The Moral Judgment of the Child.* New York: The Free Press, Macmillan.

QUINT, JOSEPH L. See Eckhart, Meister.

*RUMI. 1950. Selected, translated and with Introduction and Notes by R. A. Nicholson. London: George Allen & Unwin.

SCHECTER, DAVID E. 1959. "Infant Development." In Silvano Arieti, ed. *American Handbook of Psychiatry,* vol. 2; q.v.

SCHILLING, OTTO. 1908. *Reichtum and Eigentum in der Altkirch-lichen Literatur.* Freiburg im Breisgau: Herderische Verlags-buchhandlung.

SCHULZ, SIEGRIED. 1972. *Q Die Spruchquelle der Evangelisten.* Zurich: Theologischer Verlag.

**SCHUMACHER, E. F. 1973. *Small Is Beautiful: Economics as if People Mattered.* New York: Harper & Row, Torchbooks.

*SCHUMPETER, JOSEPH A. 1962. *Capitalism, Socialism, and De-mocracy.* New York: Harper & Row, Torchbooks.

SCHWEITZER, ALBERT. 1923. *Die Schuld der Philosophie an dem Niedergang der Kultur* [The responsibility of philosophy for the decay of culture]. Gesammelte Werke, vol. 2. Zurich: Buchclub Ex Libris.

———. 1923. *Verfall und Wiederaufbau der Kultur* [Decay and restoration of civilization]. *Gesammelte Werke,* vol. 2. Zurich: Buchclub Ex Libris.

*———. 1973. *Civilization and Ethics.* Rev. ed. Reprint of 1923 ed. New York: Seabury Press.

SIMMEL, GEORG. 1950. *Hauptprobleme der Philosophie.* Berlin: Walter de Gruyter.

SOMMERLAD, T. 1903.. *Das Wirtschaftsprogramm der Kirche des Mittelalters.* Leipzig. Quoted by Otto Schilling; q.v.

SPINOZA, BENEDICTUS DE. 1927. *Ethics.* New York: Oxford University Press.

STAEHELIN, BALTHASAR. 1969. *Haben und Sein* [Having and being]. Zurich: Editio Academica.

STIRNER, MAX. 1973. *The Ego and His Own: The Case of the Individual Against Authority.* Edited by James J. Martin; translated by Steven T. Byington. New York: Dover. (Original ed. *Der Einzige und Sein Eigentum.*)

SUZUKI, D. T. 1960. "Lectures on Zen Buddhism." In E. Fromm et al. *Zen Buddhism and Psychoanalysis;* q.v.

SWOBODA, HELMUT. 1973. *Die Qualität des Lebens.* Stuttgart: Deutsche Verlagsanstalt.

*TAWNEY, R. H. 1920. *The Acquisitive Society.* New York: Harcourt Brace.

"Technologie und Politik." *Attuell Magazin,* July 1975. Rheinbeck bei Hamburg: Rowohlt Taschenbuch Verlag.

THEOBALD, ROBERT. ed. 1966. *The Guaranteed Income: Next Step in Economic Evolution.* New York: Doubleday.

THOMAS AQUINAS. See Aquinas, Thomas.

TITMUSS, RICHARD. 1971. *The Gift Relationship: From Human Blood to Social Policy.* London: George Allen & Unwin.

*UNDERHILL, EVELYN, ed. 1956. *A Book of Contemplation the Which Is Called The Cloud of Unknowing.* 6th ed. London: John M. Watkins.

UTZ, A. F. OP. 1953. "Recht und Gerechtigkeit." In Thomas Aquinas, *Summa Theologica,* vol. 18; q.v.

YERKES, R. M., and YERKES, A. V. 1929. *The Great Apes: A Study of Anthropoid Life.* New Haven: Yale University Press.

Index

Aaron, 41

Abraham, 37, 96

activity, xxvii, 8, 13, 35, 61, 75–84, 88–90, 121, 147, 148, 167

advertising and propaganda, 113, 164, 165, 173; *see also* communications, media

alienation, xxvii, 7, 9, 21, 27, 78, 79, 92, 97, 99–100, 109–11, 134, 135–3⌐, 142, 154, 185; *see also* passivity

antagonism, 98–102; class war, xxviii, 101, 160

Aquinas, St. Thomas, xxix, 47, 80–81, 108, 108*n.*, 110

Aristippus, xxv

Aristotle, xxvi, 80, 82

Artz, Frederick B., 126

Auer, Alfons, 108, 108*n.*, 110

Augustine, St., 110, 127

authority, exercise of, 25–27, 66, 68, 70, 107, 108–9, 111, 132, 143, 176, 177–78, 179; and children, xxxii, 25, 26, 58, 64, 68, 107, 172, 177; sexual prohibitions, 66–68; *see also* bureaucracy; patriarchal society; property; rebellion and revolution

automobile, importance of, xxvii, 15, 60–61, 164, 165

Baader, Franz von, 139

Bachofen, J. J., 130

Bacon, Francis: *Novum Organum*, 160

Basho, 4, 5, 6

Basilius, 47

Bauer, Edgar, 8

Becker, Carl, 130

behaviorism, 53, 85

being (mode of existence), 8, 11, 12, 26–27, 155–57; and authority, 24–25, 25–27, 111; biblical concept, 37–47 *passim* (*see also* New Testament; Old Testament); in daily experience, 17–35, 75, 113–15; exists in the here and now, 113–14; and faith, 30, 31–32, 114; freedom and growth, xxvii, 13, 64, 65–68, 97, 157, 176–78; happiness and pleasure, 88, 102–5 *passim*, 157; and having, difference between, 3–15, 75, 87–88, 93; and having, existential, 72–73; interest, 19, 20, 23, 88, 155; knowledge, 28–30, knowledge of reality, 11, 12, 13, 20, 28, 29, 49–52, 84–87, 153; in language and speech, 11–12, 23; and learning, 18–19, 88; life, affirmation of, 4, 8, 12, 92, 97, 111–13, 156–57; philosophical concepts of, 12–13; and reading, 23–24; and remembering, 19–21, 114; security, 95–96, 97, 155, 160, 175–76; and sex, 33, 34–35, 102, 104; solidarity and union, 8, 12, 92, 98–102, 155, 175; well-being and joy, xxx, xxxi, 6, 81, 98, 102–6, 114, 156, 183–84; *see also* activity; Buddha; Eckhart, Master; Jesus;

ABOUT THE AUTHOR

ERICH FROMM was a practicing psychoanalyst and the author of such influential books as *The Art of Loving, Escape from Freedom, Beyond the Chains of Illusion, The Revolution of Hope, The Heart of Man,* and *Man for Himself.* Born in Frankfurt, Germany, in 1900, he studied at the Universities of Heidelberg and Munich and at the Psychoanalytic Institute in Berlin. He taught in Germany, and in Mexico where he was Professor of Psychoanalysis at the National University, and in the United States at Bennington College, Yale, Michigan State and New York Universities. He died in March 1980.

ABOUT THE EDITOR
OF THIS SERIES

RUTH NANDA ANSHEN, philosopher and editor, plans and edits *World Perspectives, Religious Perspectives, Credo Perspectives, Perspectives in Humanism,* and *The Science of Culture Series.* She also writes and lectures on the relationship of knowledge to the nature and meaning of man and his existence. Her book, *The Reality of the Devil: Evil in Man,* a study in the phenomenology of evil, is published by Harper & Row.